THE
VIKINGS

About the Author

Martin Arnold is Senior Lecturer in Old Norse-Icelandic Studies at Hull University. He is the author of *The Vikings: Culture and Conquest* and *The Post-Classical Icelandic Family Saga*. He was the historical consultant for the BBC Radio 4 series, *The Viking Way* (2006). He is currently co-authoring with Tom Shippey *'Laughing I Shall Die': Legends of Viking Heroes*. He lives in Scarborough.

THE
VIKINGS
A SHORT HISTORY

MARTIN ARNOLD

Cover illustrations: Front: Viking sword. Courtesy of the National Museum of Ireland. *Back:* Nineteenth-century painting by Lorenz Frolich of the Viking attack on Ordwulf's monastery in Devon in 997. Photograph courtesy of the Museum of National History at Frederiksborg Castle, Denmark/Hans Petersen.

This edition first published 2008
Published by arrangement with the Rowman & Littlefield Publishing Group
The History Press
Cirencester Road, Chalford
Stroud, Gloucestershire, GL6 8PE
www.thehistorypress.co.uk

British Library Cataloguing in Publication Data.
A catalogue record for this book is available from the British Library.

ISBN 978 0 7524 4577 9

Typesetting and origination by The History Press
Printed and bound in Great Britain
by Ashford Colour Press Ltd. Gosport, Hampshire

For my daughters
Emma and Amy

Contents

The Death of Ivar the Boneless & Viking Age History

Unconquerable king ... a terror by land and sea.

—Abbo of Fleury, *Passio Sancti Eadmundi*

One day in the summer of 1686 in the English village of Repton, Derbyshire, Thomas Walker, a farm laborer, was busy cutting hillocks near the old village church of St. Wystan when he came across an old stone wall. Tracing the wall, he discovered that it supported an enclosed mound. As he investigated further, part of the mound's roof gave way before him, revealing stone steps down to a paved floor. Walker descended and found himself inside a rectangular chamber, at the center of which was a huge stone coffin. Surrounding it were a hundred or more human skeletons, arranged so that their feet pointed toward the coffin. With some difficulty, Walker eased back the coffin's slab lid. Inside, so Walker estimated, lay a skeleton of some nine feet in length. Seemingly more amazed than frightened, Walker lifted out the massive skull and, carrying it before him, exited the chamber. Unbeknownst to Walker, what he had discovered was one of the most remarkable sites of Viking Age Europe, and what he carried in his arms was, in all probability, the skull of one of the most vicious and violent ninth-century Viking warlords, Ivar the Boneless.

The burial mound at Repton has not easily given up its secrets. Forty years after Walker's remarkable find, he recounted his adventure to a London antiquarian, but by then the skull had been lost. The antiquarian's report lacked substantiating evidence, and nothing more than the recollections of the village's old folk gave any support to Walker's story. In the centuries following, grave robbers repeatedly entered the site, and anything of obvious value was removed. In the process, the arrangement of skeletons that Walker had seen was utterly wrecked. Only in recent decades has a thorough archaeological investigation of the burial mound been undertaken. And only recently have ninth-century annals, medieval Scandinavian legends, and Walker's story been brought together and tested against the findings of archaeological research. The result has given us a credible context for what Thomas Walker found.

Exactly how we are now able to piece together the events that took place at Repton well over a thousand years ago is in itself a remarkable story. Not only that, but the detective work is an example—indeed, one of the finest examples—of historical investigation as it is now applied to the Viking Age. In this respect, it offers an exceptional insight into the difficulties that can cloud our understanding of the period. To get to the heart of the Repton story, we first need to distinguish the known, or rather the knowable, facts of the life of Ivar the Boneless from the legends that collected around him during and after his extraordinary career.

Ivar the Boneless, a Danish pagan of royal pedigree, arrived in England in 865. He had probably traveled from Dublin, which had been founded by Vikings almost thirty years earlier. Ivar had spent some ten years going back and forth from Denmark to Dublin, where he shared the rule of the city with the Norwegian Viking Olaf the White. His intention in England was to meet up with his brothers who had established their winter camp in East Anglia with an army numbering thousands, the so-named Danish Great Army. Medieval Scandinavian histories of a much later date name Ivar's brothers as Sigurd Snake-in-the-Eye, Bjorn Ironside, Halfdan, and Ubba. The brothers' purpose was nothing less than the conquest of England, which at that time was an uncomfortable composition of four different Christian kingdoms: Northumbria, Mercia, East Anglia, and Wessex.

By 865, England had already endured over seventy years of Viking attacks, beginning with the devastating assault of 793 made by Norwegian Vikings on the monastic community on the island of Lindisfarne in the far northeast of the country. The early attacks, chiefly launched against ill defended ports and treasure-laden monasteries near the coast, led to more substantial offensives from the 830s onward, when the Danes entered the scene, and were mainly concentrated in the southeast of the country.

In all probability, the reason why Danish Vikings switched their attention to the north of England was a matter of securing a firm foothold from which they could plan a coordinated campaign against English powers to the south. The place they identified for their headquarters was the chief city of Northumbria, York, once a massively fortified Roman settlement, but then an important Anglo-Saxon ecclesiastical center ruled over by a villainous usurper, King Ælla. The Vikings must have known that Northumbria was in the midst of a civil war brought about by Ælla's coup. To them, the taking of York looked militarily achievable and was, in any case, strategically vital. The prospect of uniting the commercial and political interests of Dublin with those of York would have been an added incentive, one that would certainly have attracted Ivar the Boneless.

While this, in all likelihood, was the true reasoning of Ivar and his brothers, medieval historians writing some three hundred years after the events gave a more colorful account of their motives. According to these sources, the brothers were the Ragnarssons, the sons of the legendary Ragnar Hairy Breeches. Ragnar, said to have been the long-time adversary of King Ælla of York, had been captured by him and thrown into a snake pit to die an agonizing and humiliating death. As Ragnar succumbed to the venom, he is said to have chanted his death song, which ended with the words "How the little pigs will grunt when they hear how the old boar has died." By "little pigs," he meant his sons.

The legends then say that the Ragnarssons, led by Ivar the Boneless, laid siege to York in 866, and that Ælla cheekily offered them no more land than could be covered by a horsehide. So, by slicing a hide into slender thongs, Ivar and his brothers encompassed sufficient land to establish a fortress. Ælla was duly captured and subjected to the pagan rite of the blood eagle, a brutal torture that entailed slicing open the victim's backbone, breaking apart the rib cage, and draping the lungs over the shoulders. In his final agony, Ælla was, in this way, made to resemble an eagle in flight, the bird sacred to Odin, the chief of the Viking gods. Thereafter, according to one medieval source, "Ivar held England for two years."[1]

For a more trustworthy, albeit more prosaic, account, we must turn to the *Anglo-Saxon Chronicle*. This history clearly had a bias in favor of the Wessex kings, whose mid–ninth-century kingdom spanned the south of England. Nevertheless, it has the virtue of having been compiled less than thirty years after the events of 866. What we can deduce from the *Chronicle* is that the Danish pagan generals, Ivar the Boneless, Halfdan, and Ubba, traveled to York with their Great Army. When they descended on the city, resistance proved futile, and they easily accommodated themselves inside the city's walls. The following year, King Ælla made an accord with King Osberht, his deposed predecessor, and launched a calamitous and, as it turned out, fatal counterattack.

The *Chronicle* goes on to record how the Ragnarssons proceeded to bring the midland kingdom of Mercia under their control and extend their authority eastward across East Anglia. Those who stood in their way were met with extreme brutality, as, for example, was the case with King Edmund of East Anglia, whom Ivar the Boneless and Ubba murdered in 870 for refusing to renounce Christianity and accept Viking overlordship. Some sources say that he too suffered the blood-eagle torture.

We hear no more of Ivar's deeds in the *Chronicle* after the mutilation of Edmund, but this is probably because his interests took him north to Scotland and across the Irish Sea to his one-time home of Dublin. The evidence for this depends upon equating the character named as Imhar in the authentically contemporary *Annals of Ulster* with Ivar the Boneless. The absence of Imhar from the *Annals* while Ivar was in England, and the absence of Ivar (Ingware) from the *Chronicle* while Imhar was in Scotland and Ireland make this correlation reasonable.

It would therefore appear that while Halfdan and certain other Viking generals were taking the battle for the conquest of England southward, Ivar went north. According to the thirteenth-century English historian Roger of Wendover, the brutality of Ivar and Ubba was experienced far and wide. At the Scottish monastery of Coldingham on the Firth of Forth, the abbess was so fearful of Ivar's imminent arrival that she and her nuns cut off their noses and upper lips so as to disgust their attackers and preserve their virginity. Ivar burned them alive. In Strathclyde, he was reported to have enslaved hundreds, perhaps thousands, and to have dispatched them to the Dublin slave markets. When Ivar ascended the throne of Dublin in 871, a Viking kingdom spanning mainland Britain and Ireland and ruled over by the Ragnarssons must have seemed inevitable.

Then, in 873, comes the last entry in the *Annals of Ulster* concerning Ivar/Imhar: "Imhar, king of the Norsemen of all Ireland and Britain, ended his life."[2] The question is, where?

The most significant political event in England during 873 was Halfdan Ragnarsson's dispossession of the Mercian king, Burgred. Burgred had been allowed to continue to rule his wide kingdom in 867 when he had submitted to the Ragnarssons. But six years on, Burgred had outlived his usefulness. Toward the end of 873, the Great Army made its move against Burgred and met him in open country near Repton. Burgred knew he was fighting for survival and would have made a valiant defense. But it was to no avail, and Burgred was forced to flee for his life.

Two-thirds of England now lay under direct Viking control. The Great Army would have been in a jubilant mood. It was a time for celebration, a time for taking stock. Repton, the site of their latest and most significant victory, had for centuries been home to a monastery housing both monks and nuns whose duty it was to maintain the sacred burial site of the Mercian kings. Moreover, Repton lay precisely on what has long been regarded as the dividing line between the north and the south of England. What better location could there have been to bring the Great Army to rest for the winter and plan the next steps? Yet what actually took place at Repton is highly unlikely to have been part of that plan.

It is recorded that at least four Danish generals were at Repton in 873–874, but it is not recorded that any of them died there. Yet modern archaeological evidence, let alone Thomas Walker's dramatic account, clearly indicates that someone, both of Scandinavian origin and of very high status, did die there.

Since the 1980s, the archaeologists Martin and Birthe Kjølbye-Biddle have carried out extensive research into the Repton site.[3] Their conclusions regarding the burial mound first entered by Thomas Walker are compelling. The body in the stone coffin was the only body buried intact. It was someone of considerable size. Surrounding it were the partial skeletons of roughly two hundred men and fifty women. The men were "exceptionally robust," were aged between fifteen and forty-five, and were therefore of military age. Most of them originated from Scandinavia. Viking Age artifacts and radiocarbon dating indicate that the majority of the inhumations were contemporary with the activities of the Danish Great Army. Other skeletons of an earlier date probably included those of royal Mercians of previous generations. The closing of the mound had been accompanied by an elaborate pagan ceremony, one that would appear, given the grisly find of three children and a teenage youth in a grave pit at the edge of the enclosure, to have involved human ritual sacrifice.

Nothing even closely resembling the Repton burial mound has been found outside of Scandinavia. Whoever it was that occupied the stone coffin must have been someone of the highest order. The symbolic significance entailed in the mixture of Viking warrior bones and the bones of past Mercian royalty, arranged in tributary circle around the central coffin, surely suggests an act of validation, which we might reasonably guess to have been an assertion of the primacy and legitimacy of Danish rule. There can have been few Vikings in England in 873 who could, in death, have carried such symbolic weight. Although none specify Repton, four medieval Scandinavian sources claim that Ivar died in England. Furthermore, the coincidence of dates and the evident high status of the man in the stone coffin all point to the conclusion that Repton was Ivar's last resting place.

This being so, what was it that brought about Ivar's death and the death of so many of his comrades? The battle at Repton would certainly have involved heavy casualties, but hardly any of those who died in its course can have been interred among the bodies in the mound. The archaeologists were struck by the fact that only a small number of the skeletons bore signs of trauma; in other words, very few of them had died in battle. Perhaps some of the dead had been brought to the site from other places. This would not have been an uncommon Viking practice, but, taking into account the age of those who were buried in the mound and the lack of evidence for a violent end, this too seems an inadequate explanation. It is therefore highly likely that the cause of death was disease and that a virus entered the Viking camp just at the time when victory was being celebrated. Although two Scandinavian sources claim that Ivar died of old age, two others claim that he died of a "sudden hideous disease." The likelihood is that Ivar was one among the many who succumbed at Repton through illness.

It is hardly surprising that legends accumulated around Ivar. Both from what we know and from what the medieval Scandinavian sources say, Ivar was a man of extremely unusual appearance and extreme violence, even by Viking standards. He was, in a sense, the stuff that legends are made of, albeit most often they are of the bogeyman variety. Some clue as to his character is supplied by his nickname, "the Boneless." Linguistic theories coupled with references in the legends suggest various possible interpretations. "Boneless" could mean that he was "like the wind" and therefore someone of great seafaring skill. It could refer to sexual incapacity, as is suggested in the thirteenth-century Icelandic saga of the deeds of the Ragnarssons, which states that "neither love nor lust was part of his nature." It could mean that he was paraplegic, as was claimed in another Icelandic saga. Or it could mean quite the opposite of a disability and so signify exceptional tallness, this last interpretation supporting, to some extent, Thomas Walker's nine-foot skeleton and the evidence of the huge stone coffin.

Whatever the case, the impression that Ivar left on the world soon acquired supernatural dimensions, particularly in respect to his death. Here again, there is a possible connection with Repton. One source says that Ivar was buried in "the manner of former times," which can be taken to mean the traditional pagan practice of being interred in a mound, just as was the case at Repton. But the saga life of Ivar's father also claims that Ivar commanded that he be buried near open ground vulnerable to attack and that, if this were done, no enemy would ever conquer the land. Repton, as already remarked, lies at the geographical heart of England, and the burial mound fits precisely the features of the landscape believed to have been prescribed by Ivar on his deathbed.

The power of Ivar's taboo, as set out in the saga, was said to be still potent some two hundred years later, when, in 1066, a Norwegian king and a French duke set out separately to conquer England. The former, Harald Hard-Ruler, rightly regarded as the last of the Vikings, was allegedly so perturbed by the legend that he quailed before Ivar's mound and went on to meet his doom at the hands of the English king at Stamford Bridge. The latter, William of Normandy (later William the Conqueror) was said to have taken steps to demolish Ivar's mound, so ensuring his victory over the English at Hastings and the beginning of hundreds of years of French rule. The fact that the saga locates Ivar's barrow far away in the northeast and that there are, therefore, significant geographical anomalies does not invalidate the possibility that Ivar determined the manner of his own burial and that the true location was Repton.

Setting all the evidence together—archaeological, annalistic, and legendary—it is clear that the burial mound at Repton carried far greater significance than the death of a great Viking warrior. In the mound lay one of the paladins of Danish royalty, surrounded in death by his personal bodyguard, among whom are laid the ancestry of one of the great royal houses of Anglo-Saxon England. Repton meant not only continuity with the past but also continuity into the future. The Danes would never leave.

The story of the life and death of Ivar the Boneless has historical significance for a number of reasons. In Ireland,

Ivar's absence from Dublin opened up a power vacuum into which numerous Viking rivals flowed for the next thirty years. One of the losers in this struggle for power was Ivar's brother, Halfdan. So bloody and chaotic did the situation become that the Irish, almost uniquely in concert, set aside their differences and managed to rid their country of Vikings for almost a decade and a half.

In England, the Great Army separated after Repton. Half went north back to York and set about establishing permanent settlement, and the other half went south to take on the forces of Alfred the Great of Wessex. For over eighty years, Scandinavian settlers and wave upon wave of Viking newcomers kept English forces at bay and effectively partitioned England north and south. When a second Viking Age befell England in the late tenth century, the Anglo-Scandinavian communities in the north did little to help the resistance. In due course, the Viking ambition to conquer the whole of England was achieved.

But the Repton story is interesting for other reasons than its place in Viking Age history, for it is an illustration of how reasonable historical conclusions can be drawn in respect to a time that is both remote and shrouded in legend. Some things can be known for certain about the Viking expansion: it lasted almost three hundred years, it encompassed the whole of Europe and much of the Middle East, it entailed founding new settlements right across the North Atlantic as far as the eastern seaboard of North America, and it began with the riotous assault of pagan armies on Christian Europe and ended with the establishment of Christian realms whose originators were once Vikings.

Something of the characterizing violence of the period can be deduced from the term "Viking," itself. Although a word of uncertain origin that is used in both Anglo-Saxon (*wicing*) and Scandinavian (*víkingr*) sources, and perhaps originally signifying men from Viken in southern Norway, or perhaps more generally men from the *vík*, or bay, "Viking" became synonymous with the piratical activities of Danes, Norwegians, and Swedes. Indeed, to go on a Viking raid (*í víkingr*) was something eagerly anticipated by young Scandinavian males keen to prove their manhood. The impact of this aggressive outpouring from Scandinavia cannot only be measured politically and commercially, but also linguistically. The Viking tongue, known as Old Norse, left its imprint on many European languages, nowhere more indelibly than on English, which still retains many hundreds of words from the period of the Viking settlements.

Belligerence and a strong sense of racial superiority, then, were expressive of the cultural ideals cherished by the Vikings. On hundreds of raised stones in the chiseled script form known as runes, they celebrated the deeds of their fallen heroes, and they praised the implacability of Viking leaders in stirring improvised verses known as skaldic poetry. Their death-defying resolve and lust for adventure is further enshrined in the Icelandic sagas of the thirteenth and fourteenth centuries and in the Russian chronicles of the twelfth century. Yet, for the tens of thousands of victims of the Vikings, it was their savagery and greed, as well as the incalculable damage they did to the intellectual and artistic heritage of Christian Europe, that made the greater impression. English, Irish, French, Spanish, Arab, and Greek witnesses are all in broad agreement that the Vikings were the scourge of civilization.

Nevertheless, much of our knowledge of the detail of this epic Scandinavian enterprise depends on assessing the balance of probability. Contemporary commentary, post-Viking Age medieval histories, and, where possible, archaeological evidence, all need to be weighed in the balance. As should be admitted at the outset of this history, not all the likely scenarios that are set forward here are quite as replete with compatible, or near-compatible, information as the story of the death of Ivar the Boneless. And early medieval history can only now and again claim to have scientific evidence on its side. For the main part, it is the art of the probable.

PART I

VIKING CULTURE

CHAPTER 1

From Odin to Christ

At the outset of the Viking Age in the late eighth century, Scandinavia was the last outpost of a set of religious beliefs and practices that had once been the common stock of the Germanic peoples of Northern Europe. The two chief literary sources for our knowledge of what is called Norse paganism are both known by the obscure term "edda." The *Poetic Edda* is a collection of thirty-four alliterative poems on mythological and legendary subjects, many of which have their origins in sacred rituals dating back centuries before the conversion of Scandinavia during the tenth and eleventh centuries. The *Prose Edda* is the work of the thirteenth-century Icelander Snorri Sturluson (d. 1241). It is a literary masterpiece clearly based on the *Poetic Edda*, as well as a number of other sources that have not survived. The *Prose Edda* was written in a Christian context and is presented as a repository of ancient lore for the use of poets. Set together, the eddas provide a window onto the mind-set and beliefs of the Vikings.

The Norse creation myth told of the primordial convergence of ice from the north and fire from the south, which gave rise to the first two living beings: the evil frost giant, Ymir, and the cow, Audumla, on whose milk the giant fed. From Ymir was spawned a race of giants, and from the sweat of his left armpit a man and a woman grew. As a thaw set in,

Audumla licked the melting ice, from which a powerful man emerged. In time, this man's descendants killed Ymir and used his body to fashion a cosmos of nine worlds in which lived the nine races of mortals, immortals, and monsters. Given the abominable nature of Ymir, this creation was, in itself, materially evil.

The architecture of the cosmos was arranged in three tiers. At the upper tier were the two races of the gods: the Aesir, who were the martial gods, and the Vanir, who were the fertility gods. Also in this tier were the light elves and the Hall of Slain Warriors, Valhalla, where legions of men who had won glory in life engaged in endless joyous battle in preparation for the coming of Ragnarok, the Norse apocalypse. Midgard, or Middle Earth, was the middle tier. The circumference of Midgard was bounded by the malevolent Midgard Serpent, Jormungand, which by chewing upon its own tail held the land together. Midgard was not only the abode of humans, dwarves, and dark elves, but also of giants, the most powerful and implacable enemies of the gods. In the lowest tier was Hel and Niflheim, the frozen realm of the dead, which was stalked by the fearsome dragon Nidhogg, the Corpse Tearer. Somewhere to the south of Hel was Muspell, a region of flame guarded by the giant Surt, who awaited the moment when he would lead a vast army of monstrous beings against the gods at Ragnarok.

Two bridges connected the nine worlds. Spanning the upper and middle tiers was the Flaming Bridge, Bifrost, where the god Heimdall stood ready to sound his horn at the approach of the giants. Spanning the middle and lower tier was the Echoing Bridge, Gjallarbru, watched over by the giantess Modgud, who deterred anyone from attempting either to enter or leave Hel.

The great ash tree, Yggdrasil, grew at the apex of the cosmos, and its roots encompassed all nine worlds. Yggdrasil was not only the tree of life that unified the cosmos, but it also allowed access to a higher knowledge. In what could well be the mythologized representation of a shamanic rite, it was on Yggdrasil that the chief of the gods, Odin, hung for nine days and nights in order to attain much of his magical power. The name "Yggdrasil" recalls this event and means "Odin's horse." A riot of birds and animals, some malevolent, some not, were sustained among Yggdrasil's roots and branches. Round the base of the tree sat the Norns, three mysterious women who wove the fates of gods and men. Not even the most powerful of the gods could apprehend or alter the raveling of the Norns. Conflict and chaos were the common characteristics of the fates they determined.

In the first era of the cosmos, the two races of the gods, the Aesir and the Vanir, were at war with each other, but soon after the indestructible matriarch of the Vanir was received into the company of the Aesir, the two sides were united. Thereafter, the gods cohabited, often uneasily, in the great fortress of Asgard, where Odin presided over them. Odin's chief purpose was to prepare for Ragnarok, and to this end he sent out his twelve warrior maidens, the Valkyries, to influence the course of human battles and to bring to Valhalla those most fit for defense against the giants. Odin was both wise and cunning, both protective and treacherous. He represented the aristocratic classes of Scandinavian society, reflecting their political pragmatism and their ruthlessness. It was Viking armies led by generals from royal households who went into battle under Odin's raven banner.

Next in importance, or at least of greatest prominence, were Thor, Frey and his sister Freyja, and Loki. Thor's role in the myths was that of henchman, and his character was clearly a hyperbole of male strength and virility. It was Thor who was the scourge of the giants and the tribe of rapacious female monsters, the trolls. Judging from the numerous neck pendants and amulets that have been found representing Thor's hammer, Mjollnir, it was Thor who was the favorite among Viking foot soldiers, farmers, and ordinary folk. Frey and Freyja were the chief fertility gods and, as such, were typically depicted in the myths as being embroiled in sexual intrigues, often of a deeply reprehensible nature. In the actualities of religious practice, they were associated with fecundity and childbearing, and the farming and fishing communities of Scandinavian society would also have invoked their power over the harvests of land and sea.

Loki was in many ways the most intriguing of the gods. Of mixed giant and Aesir parentage, Loki's loyalties were ever in doubt. He was sexually indiscriminate and responsible for siring the three most destructive of the gods' enemies, the so-called monstrous brood of Hel, the Midgard Serpent, and the apocalyptic wolf, Fenrir. Much of Loki's career was spent trying to avert the potential disasters that he, personally, had brought to bear upon the gods. But Loki could also be spiteful. In the mythological sequence leading directly to Ragnarok, Loki was personally responsible for the death of the most beloved of the gods, Odin's favorite son, Baldur. For his wickedness, the gods punished Loki by binding him beneath rocks with the intestines of his own son and setting a snake above him, whose venom dripped onto his face. Only the ministrations of his wife, Sif, who gathered the venom in a bowl, saved him from perpetual torture. At the outset of Ragnarok, Loki would break free from his fetters in order to play out his final treachery by leading his monstrous brood against the Aesir. Loki was that mercurial supernatural being, the trickster god, and, as such, he was not the subject of cultic reverence.

Norse mythology was typically violent, often lewd and sexualized, and in its sense of the ultimate destiny of things—its eschatology—doom laden. The central drama was the conflict between the gods and the giants, in which the gods functioned as life-affirming principles, while the giants functioned as life-denying principles. This is apparent in the myth that appears early on in the mythological cycle known as the Masterbuilder Tale, which tells how a mason of great skill offers to make the walls of the gods' stronghold, Asgard, impregnable within eighteen months. The only payment he will accept is the goddess Freyja, the sun, and the moon. The gods deliberate, knowing that such a price would bring about their extinction. Eventually, Loki convinces them that they should agree to the payment, but only on the seemingly impossible condition that the job should be completed in one winter, so guaranteeing, he argues, a great deal of the mason's effort for free. The mason grudgingly accepts these terms but asks that he be allowed to use his horse. The gods find no objection to this seemingly modest request, and a contract is duly made.

It then transpires that the mason's horse is a stallion of phenomenal strength, and that with its help the mason will complete the fortification according to the terms agreed, with all the lethal consequences. In panic, the gods turn to Loki and demand a solution. Loki's response is to transform himself into a mare and lure the stallion away. The mason is infuriated, and in his wild show of temper, he reveals his true identity as a rock giant. The gods summon Thor who returns to Asgard and smashes in the giant's skull with his hammer. Some months later, Loki reappears with an eight-legged colt in tow, the product of his dalliance with the mason's stallion, which he gives to Odin. But the walls of Asgard remain half built, the gods forever vulnerable, and with the contract between the gods and the giants broken, the air between them is poisoned for all time.

Exactly how this myth relates to cultic practices is uncertain, but its themes of incompleteness, vulnerability, and the threat of extinction might well be regarded as an abstract commentary on mortal anxieties. Indeed, many critics have attempted to explain Norse myth in terms of an abstraction of a perceived conflict between man and his environment, between culture and nature. Certainly Scandinavian farmers and fishermen and Viking adventurers on the high seas would have been only too aware of the precariousness of life. Yet, in early societies, threats were not only posed by the difficulties of eking out a living and providing for dependants, but also by rivals from outside the group and, perhaps just as often, within the group. The obligations of family and tribal loyalty, hierarchical codes, and the imperatives that went along with collective survival were also sewn into the rich tapestry of the myths. Culture and nature personifications are certainly there, but so are a great many other complexities concerning human experiences, aspirations, and fears.

Norse mythology was perhaps not conceived of in terms of the sequential narrative that was set forward in Snorri Sturluson's *Prose Edda*, and for the reality of its expression, one must turn to the *Poetic Edda*, much of which is tantalizingly obscure. An unambiguous cycle of myths, with an orthodoxy of events and character traits, may have been accomplished in time, but this development was cut short by the Christian conversion of Scandinavia. Contact throughout the Viking Age with Christian Europe may also have influenced Norse mythology, and some scholars, rightly or wrongly, have been tempted to see such episodes as the crucifixion of Odin on Yggdrasil as a borrowing from Christian myth. Nevertheless, there is much else that is wholly unique, and it is quite possible to make certain general observations about the distinct character of Norse paganism.

What makes Norse myth different from, for example, Christian myth is that it offers no explicit moral guidance and no comforting notions of a better life hereafter.Members of the Norse pantheon often behave in ways that suggest what one ought not to do rather than what one should do, and such ethical principles as are implied are invariably concerned with the here and now. Self-denial or sacrifice in service of some higher noble cause is a rare feature of the behavior of the gods, and in this sense, Norse myth is deeply materialistic. Enemies must be vanquished, land and goods must be protected and added to, matches must be made, and life must be endured with heroic fortitude.

However, in all cases, the final outcome is the obvious one, for this ceaseless struggle will lead ultimately to extinction, to a collective or personal Ragnarok.The clearest expression of what this fatalism meant in terms of an ethic by which men—particularly men—should live is found among the verses uttered by Odin for the guidance of warriors, in the eddic poem "Sayings of the High One" (*Hávamál*):

> Cattle die, kinsmen die,
> the self must also die,

but glory never dies,

for the man who is able to achieve it.

Cattle die, kinsman die,

the self must also die,

I know one thing which never dies,

the reputation of each dead man.[1]

As is consistent with Norse myth, there is no sense in this philosophy of spiritual obligation, no sense of inward reflection, and no transcendence. All that mattered was reputation, and, this being the case, all that mattered was the opinion of others. This was the warrior's creed, and pagan religious, ethical, and social values all lent legitimacy and urgency to the plainer and uglier motivations of ferocious greed that underpinned the Viking expansion.

The savagery and ritual slaughter that attended the actual practice of Norse paganism was well attested by eyewitness reports, and much of what was reported has, in more recent times, been corroborated by archaeological evidence. The monk and historian Adam of Bremen, writing in or around 1075 about the continuance of cultic rites among the Swedes, told of the horrors that were reported to him regarding ceremonies at the gilded pagan temple at Uppsala. Every nine years, wrote Adam, a solemn feast was dedicated to the gods Odin, Thor, and Frey, and everyone in the kingdom was obliged to send offerings, whether Christian or pagan.During the feasting, nine males of every species were ritually sacrificed, and after the mass sacrifices, the putrefying bodies of dogs and horses were hanged alongside the human victims in a sacred grove. Adam also referred to "manifold and unseemly" rituals that were so appalling that he could not bring himself to describe them.[2] Adam's Christian outrage may have colored his prose, but the evidence for Uppsala having once been a major sacred site for Norse pagans is apparent to this day in the shape of the three large fifth-century burial mounds that were once dedicated to the gods.

Adam was not alone in recording or recalling the ghastly nature of such gatherings in Scandinavia, and Thietmar of Merseberg, a German writing in 1016, some fifty years after the conversion of Denmark, reported that at Lejre in Sjaelland, major cultic ceremonies had also taken place every nine years. At these, ninety-nine humans and a similar number of horses, dogs, and cocks were sacrificed. A large hall, which was the seat of royal power, and an open-air stone setting of some 260 feet in length in the shape of a ship have been excavated at Lejre, and both of these are likely to have been locations for the rituals described by Thietmar.

The Arab diplomat Ibn Fadlan, who encountered a Viking war party on the Volga in the early tenth century, wrote an even more explicit and, in this case, wholly credible account of pagan barbarism. The particular ceremony that Ibn Fadlan witnessed was the ship cremation of one of the Viking chieftains. To accompany him into the afterlife, a young slave girl was selected, and for several days she was fed intoxicants that left her in a state of euphoria. As the cremation approached, the slave girl was sent round the tents of the dead man's comrades, where she was, one after the other, ceremonially raped, seemingly as a gesture of respect to the departed. The girl soon entered a visionary state, at which point she claimed to be able to see her late master and her deceased ancestors. Ibn Fadlan's description of what took place next is shocking:

Then men came with shields and sticks. She was given a cup of nabid [an intoxicant]; she sang at taking it and drank. The interpreter told me that she in this fashion bade farewell to all her girl companions. Then she was given another cup; she took it and sang for a long time while the old woman incited her to drink up and go into the pavilion where her master lay. I saw that she was distracted; she wanted to enter the pavilion but put her head between it and the boat. Then the old woman seized her head and made her enter the pavilion and entered with her. Thereupon the men began to strike with sticks on the shields so that her cries should not be heard and the other slave girls would not be frightened and seek to escape death with their masters. Then six men went into the pavilion and each had intercourse with the girl. Then they laid her at the side of her master; two held her feet and two her hands; the old woman known as the Angel of Death re-entered and looped a cord around her neck and gave the crossed ends to the two men for them to pull. Then she approached her with a broad-bladed dagger, which she plunged between her ribs repeatedly, and the men strangled her with the cord until she was dead.[3]

The ritual ended with the cremation of the girl's body alongside that of her master's.

The description of the suttee of the slave girl on the Volga may not be typical in every detail of pagan rites throughout the Viking world, but, in its essential components, it was. The sexual abuse of female slaves was observed by Ibn Fadlan at other assemblies of Vikings, where they were not above gratifying their lust in public, apparently without censure or surprise. Similarly, the sacrifice of both female and male slaves at Viking funerals was widely reported and is amply evidenced by archaeological finds across Scandinavia. The burial ships that have been excavated at Oseberg and Gokstad in Norway both entailed the ritual murder of slaves, and at Stengarde in Denmark, a tenth-century master and slave burial has been unearthed, the latter of whom had had his feet tied together and had been decapitated.

Across Scandinavia, a ritual sacrifice ceremony was known as a *blót*, a blood offering. The creation of the world from the body of the frost giant Ymir and the death of the beloved god Baldur were both calendar events for blood offerings. A *blót* might, on the one hand, be a relatively low-key affair at which farm animals were slaughtered, or, on the other, it might be a grand ritual at which humans were sacrificed, either by hanging, stabbing, drowning, or the breaking of the backbone. Weighted human remains have been found in Scandinavian bogs, and these are believed to have been the victims of such rituals. Cannibalism may also have played a part in certain of these ceremonies. At an important *blót*, the bodies of human victims were cut open and the bones split in order to take auguries known as *hlaut*. This word has its equivalent in modern English as "lot," as in "one's lot," and relates to this process of casting lots to interpret the future.

Norse paganism was a major part of preconversion Viking Age culture. It was, for example, central to the operation of the law, which was presided over by a priestly cast, who were, at one and the same time, the chieftains or royal designates, although certain fertility rites may have been conducted by priestesses. The senior authority in both the law and religious practice was the king, who may himself have been regarded as a divine being. Invocations to the gods and the letting of animal blood were key aspects of the solemnization of the legal proceedings and juridical assemblies known as Things.

Yet, except in certain areas where cults thrived and were sanctioned by royal authority, such as at Uppsala, religious practice was optional. There was no particular obligation placed on individuals to revere one god more than any other; indeed, there was no obligation to revere any god at all. A farmer may have dedicated a particular field or nearby hill to Thor, a chieftain may have dedicated his horse to Frey, and a sea captain may have dedicated his boat to Odin, and whilst others were expected to respect these sanctifications, they were not expected to share the same conviction. Despite its obviously grotesque ceremonies, Norse paganism can be regarded as a tolerant religion, which, unlike Christianity, did not have any missionary impulse. However, this does not mean that its adherents were not zealous in their faith and violently resentful of any imposed alternative.

The conversion of Scandinavia and the Viking colonies elsewhere was a patchy and, for the most part, protracted affair. Where contact with Christian communities was most intense, such as in the foreign settlements, conversion and assimilation was quite a rapid process, but conversion did not always hold firm. There are many recorded instances of apostasy, of backsliding into the old ways. One monk who was still in despair at pagan recidivism in the early twelfth century summed up what was a common situation:

> [They] seem to honour the Christian faith only when things go according to their wishes and luck is on their side [but when] storm winds are against them ... then they persecute the Christian faith that they claim to honour.[4]

Whether Christian and pagans in and around Viking settlements could always cohabit as good neighbors is highly doubtful, and the collisions of faith and cultural tradition were a fact of life throughout the Viking Age. In Viking Age York, in northern England, for instance, Christian conversion was taking place by the end of the ninth century, yet the last of the Viking kings of York, the notorious Eirik Bloodaxe, was still a pagan in the mid-tenth century, when he was ousted by his unhappy subjects. The eddic poem "The Lay of Eirik" celebrates Eirik's arrival in Valhalla as one of Odin's elite warriors.

The greater the contact the Vikings had with Christian communities, the sooner they were likely to convert, notwithstanding that baptism was often accepted quite cynically in order to improve trade relations or to gain political respectability, or, in places where territorial battles were being fought, simply to buy time. But in the Scandinavian homelands, where traditions were better insulated against outside influences, the grip of Norse paganism proved difficult for Christian missionaries to break.

Efforts to convert the Scandinavians had begun long before the Viking Age, but with no success. The conversion of the Danish king Harald Klak in the 820s appeared to be a breakthrough for the church, but Harald's subjects took a different view and drove him from power. The Frankish missionary Anskar (d. 865) had some modest success in Sweden when he was granted permission to build a church at the trading center of Birka, but, again, it did not last. Anskar, however, was resolute, and when Danish Vikings fell victim to a plague after an attack on Paris, Anskar managed to convince King Horik that it was the doing of the sainted spirit of St. Germain. Horik promptly returned the booty that had been seized and granted permission for churches to be built at Ribe and Hedeby, and Anskar was subsequently able to revive the Swedish church at Birka. However, within less than a generation, these concessions had been withdrawn.

It was not until the middle decades of the tenth century that firm progress was made with the conversion of King Hakon the Good of Norway and, shortly afterward, King Harald Bluetooth of Denmark. Both men appreciated the political capital that could be gained from entering mainstream Christian Europe, and both set about rebranding pagan sites and ceremonies in Christian terms. Yet, while the conversion of the Danes was largely completed by the end of the century, the Norwegians continued to take rather more persuading.

The opportunistic Norwegian Viking warlord Olaf Tryggvason, who clawed his way to the throne of Norway in 995, had no patience with those who stuck to the old ways. Underlying Olaf's missionary zeal was his desire to unite Norway under his rule. Convert or die was his message, and dispossession or death was the outcome for those who did not appreciate his sincerity. In the case of Iceland, which not only shunned Christianity but also kings, Olaf dispatched the homicidal Thangbrand, whose mission included beating people to death with his giant crucifix. By the year 1000, Olaf had achieved what he wanted, but he had made so many enemies along the way that he did not survive the year to enjoy the benefits of being the ruler of a Christian kingdom. Backsliding and disintegration were very soon in full swing.

Less than two decades after Olaf Tryggvason's death, another Olaf, Olaf Haraldsson, picked up where his namesake had left off. Blinding and mutilation were Olaf Haraldsson's highly effective evangelical persuaders. Less effective were Olaf's political stratagems, and in 1030 he was outnumbered four to one by an army of 14,000 Norwegian farmers, who preferred to be ruled from England by the Danish king, Cnut the Great. Yet there was consolation in death, for the church that he had so assiduously championed posthumously transformed Olaf into St. Olaf.

With Denmark, Norway, and Iceland all incorporated into Catholic Europe, the outstanding problem remained Sweden. King Olof Skötkonung had converted, perhaps as early as the late tenth century, and had brought a rather precarious unity to the country, but nothing of this survived his death in 1022, despite a succession of Christian kings. Christian missionaries were, however, getting bolder, and in the 1060s they began wandering around pagan sites in Sweden, pulverizing the edifices they found. They were fortunate to escape with their lives, because the Swedes were self-evidently the most obstinate of pagans, as became apparent in the 1080s when a large number of them elected Blót Svein, or Svein the Sacrificer, as their leader. It would take until the early twelfth century for Sweden to become a united Christian realm.

The impact of the conversion on the Scandinavians can be measured in a number of different ways. Culturally, it could have been nothing less than traumatic, for it meant that long-held traditions were not only made obsolete but were also deemed blasphemous and heretical. This could explain to some extent why Icelanders of the Middle Ages invested so much of their energy in preserving or redrafting the sacred literature of Norse paganism and in writing sagas about the deeds of their forebears prior to the conversion. Although this widespread activity was clearly not a case of backsliding in the sense of some late desire to revive Norse paganism, it was nonetheless a little ironic, as only with Christianity came literacy and the inexhaustible possibilities of the Roman alphabet that so enthralled the saga writers.

The changes in religious practice had a significant impact on Scandinavian society. Something of this can be gleaned from twelfth-century Icelandic histories, which recorded the bans that came into force when the country converted almost overnight in the year 1000. Firstly, there was to be no more of the infanticidal practice of exposing unwanted infants to the bitter elements. Secondly, there should be no more public sacrifices, although private sacrifices would be allowed to continue for a brief period. Thirdly, there should be no more eating of horseflesh, a practice that was associated with the sacrifice of horses in pagan rituals. The effect of these bans would have been deeply felt at the time, and certain tensions arose in the communities as a consequence, but nevertheless, any dissatisfaction that was caused did not outlast much more than a single generation.

The greatest impact by far was political. In monarchic mainland Scandinavia, the conversion meant that greater authority was centered on kings and away from local chieftains. This was clearly one of the chief incentives underlying the actions of such converts as Olaf Tryggvason. Christian Viking kings saw no limit to their ambitions, for, as Christians, they could seek the mandate of popes and in this way legitimize their territorial conquests, even after the fact, as was the case in the eleventh century with the conqueror of England, Cnut the Great. The Christian conversion simplified Viking relations with Europe and in certain ways normalized them, but for a time it also magnified the possibilities for aggressive expansion.

At the level of ordinary society, however, few would have felt that much had changed. Slaves continued to be slaves, despite the church's teachings that manumission was charitable and godly. Indeed, slave trading—one of the chief currencies of the Vikings—only diminished for economic reasons, and the keeping of slaves was not finally abolished until the twelfth century, except in Sweden, where slave ownership was widespread for another two hundred years, even among the clergy.

Similarly, gender inequalities remained much as they had been, although there is some literary evidence to suggest that the role of women in society may have diminished even further. This can be seen particularly in the Norse tradition of the "strong woman" as she was depicted before and after the conversion. In traditional lore, women such as Brynhild the Valkyrie, who wrought the murder of her lover Sigurd the Dragon Slayer, and Sigurd's wife, the formidable Gudrun, were much admired. But according to the lights of Christian theology, which emphasized the virtuous role of women as helpmeets and domestics, viragoes like Brynhild and Gudrun were anachronisms.

The gradual move from Odin to Christ during the Viking Age was obviously a desirable one for all concerned, socially and politically. For those in the upper echelons of Scandinavian society and for Viking settlers throughout Europe, more often than not, conversion simply meant more profit and more power and so was entered into without any need for spiritual revelation. But Christian Vikings were in one way preferable to their pagan forebears, as they were less likely to attack holy places. However, by that time, there was little remaining that had not already been either destroyed or damaged. Where

Viking vandalism had impacted on monastic libraries, the loss was permanent.

Yet there is also no doubt that, for some, conversion was absolutely sincere. There are over two thousand runic monuments in Scandinavia dating from the late tenth century to the early twelfth century that testify to a clear understanding of the spiritual dimensions of the Christian message. For the majority of Norse pagans, when Ragnarok came, it was not as a sudden apocalypse but as a slow acceptance of a set of values that, at least in principle, were more humane, more coherent, and, importantly, more European. These words from the eddic poem "Seeress' Prophecy" could either signify a dark dread of aggressive Christian evangelizing or a yearning for its intervention:

Then the powerful, mighty one, he who rules over everything,
Will come from above, to the judgement place of the gods.[5]

CHAPTER 2

The Warrior's Way

In the east of Iceland, in the late tenth century, the tensions between the bothers Helgi and Grim Droplaugarson and their overbearing neighbor Helgi Asbjarnarson eventually turned into open and bloody conflict. It was wintertime, and snow was thick on the ground when Helgi Asbjarnarson set an ambush for the brothers and their companions, making sure that he considerably outnumbered them. During the initial attack, both Grim Droplaugarson and Helgi Asbjarnarson were injured, the former very badly, the latter sufficient to make him sit out the fight. Surrounded by Helgi Asbjarnarson's men, two of whom are named here as Hjarrandi and Ozur, Helgi Droplaugarson was at first unaware of his brother's injuries.

Helgi Droplaugarson's shield got badly hacked, and he saw that it would be no use to him with things the way they were. Then Helgi showed his skill in arms and threw up his shield and sword and caught the sword in his left hand and struck at Hjarrandi, hitting him on the thigh. But the sword did not cut after it reached the bone, and it glanced off down into the hollow of the knee, and he was disabled by that wound. But at that moment Hjarrandi struck at Helgi, but he warded off the blow with his shield, and the sword sprang off it into his face and onto his row of teeth, taking off the lower lip.

Then Helgi said, 'I was never beautiful, but you've made little improvement.'

He then felt with his hand and thrust his beard into his mouth and bit on it. But Hjarrandi went down to the base of the snowdrift and sat down.

Then Helgi saw that Grim, his brother, had fallen; they who had attacked him were all dead, but Grim was mortally wounded.

Then Helgi took the sword that Grim had owned and said, 'Now has fallen the man to whom I was best disposed. My namesake must surely wish that we should not just part like that.'

And Helgi then made for where Helgi Asbjarnarson was sitting, and he happened to come down just opposite Ozur.

'There you stand, Ozur,' said Helgi, 'and I'm not going to guard myself against you, because you sprinkled me with water at my namegiving.'

Then Ozur had to think quickly of what to do, because the death of either one of the two Helgis was imminent. Ozur's solution was that he lunged at Helgi Droplaugarson with a spear, so that it went right into him.

Helgi walked forward onto the spear and said to Ozur, 'Now you have betrayed me.'

Ozur saw that Helgi was moving towards him and would reach him with the sword. Then he pushed the spear and everything with it away from him. Then he turned the spear downwards into the ground and then let go of it.

Then Helgi said, when he saw that he could not reach him, 'Now I delayed while you, on the other hand, hurried.'

He then staggered off, out onto the snow, and thus ended the life of Helgi Droplaugarson.[1]

Given that at least two hundred years separate the composition of *The Saga of the Sons of Droplaug* and the events it describes, we must grant the likelihood that creative imaginings have influenced the telling of the story. Helgi Droplaugarson is presented as the model hero: he does not fear death, he seems impervious to pain, he is suicidally loyal, and he is always ready with a pithy comment, irrespective of the gravity of the situation. He is the epitome of the warrior who dies the glorious death and whose good reputation will live after him. In this sense, he is as much an ideal as a reality.

Whether or not we are convinced by the author's presentation of Helgi's character, there is something grimly realistic about his last stand, much of which accords precisely with what we know about the use of Viking Age weaponry in close-quarter combat. In this deadly contest, both sides were armed with swords or spears, and it can be presumed that all the combatants had shields. Shields were typically circular, were made of softwood, and measured approximately three feet in diameter. They were reinforced at the rim with iron or leather trim, and at the center was a raised iron boss intended as a deflector and as protection for the handgrip on the reverse side. Helgi's shield rapidly became unserviceable, and in the encounter with Hjarrandi, the protective boss probably worked to his disadvantage by causing his attacker's sword blow to deflect into his face. From this we can also conclude that Helgi was not wearing a helmet with a face guard and that he probably had nothing more than a conical leather headpiece to protect him.

Helgi's sword also seems to have suffered. His strike against Hjarrandi failed to cut deep enough to completely neutralize his opponent, and as a consequence he suffered a counter-blow. Knowing that his own sword was no longer effective, Helgi retrieved Grim's sword. Swords in the Viking Age were much-prized weapons, but only a few, usually imported from the master smithies of Francia, were of the carbon-steel variety. Helgi's sword would have been made of iron and easily blunted. Swords were not fencing but slashing weapons, and a chief target was an opponent's legs. If, as was likely in a planned ambush, the attackers wore protective clothing, such as a thick leather apron-style jerkin (although probably not the chain-mail equivalent worn by Viking leaders), then a blow to the legs was a quick way of ending any threat. This was precisely what Helgi intended to achieve against Hjarrandi.

Spears were used alongside a range of other missiles, including arrows, and were often launched in salvos at the ranks of the opposition, but in close-quarter combat they were useful as long-reach stabbing weapons. When Ozur stabbed at Helgi and impaled him, he did so knowing that Helgi was unprotected. Yet to let go of a spear could have the unintended consequence of providing the target with an additional weapon. Although this was obviously not the case when Ozur delivered Helgi his deathblow, Ozur nevertheless realized that Helgi still needed to be put beyond reach, and the protruding spear gave him the purchase to render Helgi harmless.

One weapon not mentioned specifically in the encounter is the battleax, although it was probably this weapon that caused so much damage to Helgi's shield. An iron ax could be the light hand ax, wielded with one hand, or the broad-blade ax, wielded with both hands. Given the scarcity of good swords, the battle-ax was the weapon of choice for Viking infantrymen. Beautifully decorated axes have been discovered, indicating that they were not only implements of violence but also valued possessions. The battle-ax was, of course, a hacking weapon, and its effectiveness depended on the muscle power invested in a great arching swing. It also depended on the accuracy of the swing, for to miss the mark could place the wielder off balance and render him vulnerable. A particularly spectacular use of the ax is described in *The Saga of Burnt Njal* and concerns the athletic vengeance taken by Skarp-Hedin against his enemy Thrain.

> Skarp-Hedin jumped up as soon as he had tied his shoe, and hoisted his axe. He raced down straight towards the river. A huge sheet of ice had formed a low hump on the other side of the channel. Thrain and his men had stopped on the middle of this hump. Skarp-Hedin made a leap and cleared the channel between the ice-banks, steadied himself, and at once went into a slide: the ice was glassy-smooth, and he skimmed along as fast as a bird.
>
> Thrain was then about to put on his helmet. Skarp-Hedin came swooping down on him and swung at him with his axe. The axe crashed down on his head and split it down to the jaw-bone, spilling the backteeth on to the ice. It all happened so quickly that no-one had time to land a blow on Skarp-Hedin as he skimmed past at great speed.[2]

Skarp-Hedin's vengeance had something of the character of that taken by a Hollywood action hero, but it was probably not unique. There were instances of Viking war bands in Scandinavia traveling to battle equipped with skis and skates, and Vikings mounted on horseback could also have achieved similarly devastating results.

As Helgi Droplaugarson's fateful encounter shows, a close-quarter combatant was only as good as the equipment he carried. For this reason, attacking moves were usually preferred to defensive ones. The first blow could often settle the outcome, and in order to achieve this advantage, a mixture of low cunning and brute strength—of Odin and Thor—was required. This was Skarp-Hedin's resort, and it was also one that characterized the broader tactics of Viking armies.

Viking armies before the latter part of the tenth century were not standing armies, nor were they constituted wholly of professional soldiers. A share in any booty or the chance to seize land and start a new life outside Scandinavia was what held an army together, although a central elite or a particular war party may have been bound to each other by family ties or other traditional loyalties. Some regarded Viking expeditions as seasonal affairs and as something to be fitted in between crop sowing and harvest. Others spent several years in service of one or more Viking warlords. For a few, being a Viking was a lifelong profession.

The Vikings did not favor large battlefield encounters, and although this could not always be avoided, the preferred strategies were the surprise attack and the siege. The year-long siege of Paris in 885–886 was one of the Vikings' less successful forays, and their vast army was held at bay on the River Seine by a mere two hundred Franks garrisoned inside the fortification spanning the river. According to Abbo of Fleury, the Vikings grew impatient after six months and decided to apply a little science to the task.

> The Danes then make, astonishing to see, three huge machines, mounted on sixteen wheels—monsters made of immense oak trees bound together; upon each was placed a battering ram, covered with a high roof—in the interior and on the sides of which could be placed and concealed, they said, sixty men armed with their helmets.[3]

Although the siege ultimately failed and the Vikings went on instead to lay waste to Frankish territories east and north of Paris, this is a fine example of how they could summon considerable engineering skills to achieve their ends.

When the need arose, broader battle strategies had to be carefully devised. Snorri Sturluson, in his history of the Norwegian kings, *Heimskringla*, told how at the Battle of Stiklestad in 1030, Olaf Haraldsson set out his plans to overcome an army four times larger than his own.[4] Olaf deployed his men around three standard-bearers, with his own contingent taking the center ground. Olaf calculated that camaraderie would be best encouraged by dividing his men according to their place of origin; thus, with him were the Norwegians, to his right were the southern Swedes, and to his left were the northern Swedes.

Olaf's basic idea was to string out his battle lines in these three battalions to avoid being surrounded. Then, in what was probably the common battle tactic of Viking armies, Olaf was to signal a headlong charge into the opposing ranks, in the hope of taking them by surprise and provoking panic. In every respect, Olaf's plan was probably the best possible one under the circumstances, and for a short while it seemed it might work. However, in the end, force of numbers triumphed; Olaf was killed, and his army was routed.

Dividing an army into battalions not only encouraged loyalties but also allowed flexibility. The *Annals of Ulster* record how, in 918, Vikings from Ireland, under the leadership of a certain Ragnall, fell into an evenly matched, pitched battle with the Scots. Ragnall made the most of what could be done with his four battalions, including setting a trap for the unwary Scots.

The foreigners of Waterford, i.e. Ragnall, king of the Danes, and the two jarls, Oitir and Gragabai, forsook Ireland and proceeded afterwards against the men of Scotland. The men of Scotland, moreover, moved against them and they met on the bank of the Tyne in Northern Saxland. The heathens formed themselves into four battalions: a battalion with Gothfrith grandson of Ímhar, a battalion with the two jarls, and a battalion with the young lords. There was also a battalion in ambush with Ragnall, which the men of Scotland did not see. The Scotsmen routed the three battalions which they saw, and made a very great slaughter of the heathens, including Oitir and Gragabai. Ragnall, however, then attacked in the rear of the Scotsmen, and made slaughter of them, although none of their earls was cut off. Nightfall caused the battle to be broken off.[5]

Ferocity and fearlessness were the main qualities required of a Viking warrior, and Viking warlords would have been keen to recruit those particularly violent individuals known as berserks. These men were clearly psychopaths who could rouse themselves into what was called the berserker rage at the onset of hostilities. At the Battle of Hafrsfjord in or around 885, the fleet of King Harald Finehair of Norway was confronted by a crew of berserks who "bellowed" and "shrieked" and "shook their weapons" as battle was joined. The turning point of the battle came when Haklang, the berserk leader, was killed. Men such as Haklang would have taken the forward and exposed positions in the "swine wedge," where as many as thirty men took up a triangular formation, thus resembling the shape of a pig's snout. Their aim was to advance in close quarter against the enemy shield wall with the intention of shattering it. Few would choose to stand against a raging berserk.

During the latter part of the tenth century, Viking armies became more structured. Norway and Denmark were by this time becoming distinct and wealthy nation-states that had much to fear from each other. Standing armies were required, both to secure national borders and to prosecute a war of conquest against England. The Danish king, Harald Bluetooth (d. ca. 998), established garrisons throughout his Danish territories known as the Trelleborg ring forts. The largest of these circular wooden fortresses was at Aggersborg, and at 780 feet in diameter, it could accommodate up to eight thousand men. With families and tradesmen living in buildings outside the ramparts, there could have been a population of going on twenty thousand at Aggersborg alone. Legend has it that Harald Bluetooth also sponsored a particularly focused Viking brotherhood known as the Jomsvikings, who had three hundred longships at their disposal at a secret stone fortress in the Baltic, although no evidence has been found to support this claim.

Generally speaking, Viking armies were no better equipped and no better trained than the armies they confronted, and records even suggest that when it came to an equal fight, the Vikings lost more often than they won. Paradoxically, their strength lay in what might usually be regarded as a weakness—that is to say, in their lack of military coherence and continuity.

Vikings could assemble in large force, launch a lightning strike against a relatively poorly defended target such as a monastery, and then melt away before significant opposition could arrive, only to regroup elsewhere. Before Viking armies established themselves as permanent features on foreign soil, they came and went from the sea, where few could equal their maritime skills. Their capacity to maneuver men and supplies around coastal waters and through inland waterways remained crucial to Viking expeditions throughout the Viking Age. The real key to their success, then, was the longship.

The main purpose of the longship was to deliver warriors to land. This lethal practicality was enhanced by the elegance of the longship design. It had a terrifying beauty. In 1015, when Cnut of Denmark set out with a fleet of two hundred longships on what turned out to be his successful conquest of England, a monk from the monastery of St. Omer in Flanders watched in amazement.

> So great, also, was the ornamentation of the ships, that the eyes of the beholders were dazzled, and to those looking from afar they seemed of flame rather than of wood. For if at any time the sun cast the splendour of its rays among them, the flashing of arms shone in one place, in another the flame of suspended shields. Gold shone on the prows, silver also flashed on the variously shaped ships. So great, in fact, was the magnificence of the fleet, that if its lord had desired to conquer any people, the ships alone would have terrified the enemy, before the warriors whom they carried joined battle at all. For who could look upon the lions of the foe, terrible with the brightness of gold, who upon the men of metal, menacing with golden face, who upon the dragons burning with pure gold, who upon the bulls on the ships threatening death, their horns shining with gold, without feeling any fear for the king of such a force?[6]

Vikings were no less impressed than the monk by their extraordinary craft. Composers of the complex verses known as skaldic poetry were often called upon to celebrate their patron's deeds. This verse commemorates the longship of King Harald Hard-Ruler of Norway as it carried the king out across the ingress to the Baltic to make war against the Danes.

Much ill will suffer oaken
Oarlocks, ere by rowers
Seventy sweeps from stormy
Sea be lifted sithen:
Onward, Northmen urge the
Iron-mailed great dragon,
Like as, with outspread wings, an
Eagle, on hailstruck sea-stream.[7]

The evolution of the longship can be traced back thousands of years to the primitive dugout canoes that once plied Scandinavia's fjords and inland lakes. From the beginning of the first millennium, longer, sleeker boats were made using lapstrake planking, which tapered to a beaked prow and stern on which were carved fearsome animals. By the fifth century, a boat featuring a clinker-built hull with a rudder fixed on the starboard side was in use. Bronze Age art depicts a dragon guarding over these craft, an image that later came to symbolize the warlike intent of the longship. Finally, a T-shaped keel was developed that ran in perfect symmetry from prow to stern. The longship and its predecessors were clearly not designed to plough the waves but to ride them. To this end, the longship rarely had a draft of more than four to five feet.

Exactly when Scandinavian shipbuilders added sail to their craft is not known for certain, but there are indications that sail was in widespread use by the early eighth century; indeed, one Roman commentator reports northern Germanic raiders using sail as early as the late fifth century. Modest sail craft may have been in use among Scandinavians hundreds of years before the Viking Age.

A single square-rigged sail on a ninth- or tenth-century longship could be as large as one hundred square yards, and in a favorable wind, a longship could achieve an average speed of ten knots, under which circumstances a crossing from Norway to England could be achieved in a day and a night. In less favorable conditions, when, for example, tacking was required against a headwind, an average speed of two knots was more likely. Rowing power was the necessary alternative to sail and was, of course, essential on rivers. A Viking longship coming to land with hostile intentions could readily furl its sail and unstep its central mast, so allowing passage under bridges and, by deception, gaining an element surprise.

The main class of warship was the dragon ship (*drakkar*), so called because of the dragon's head carved on the beaked prow and because of its reptilian appearance. One of the scuttled longships recovered from Roskilde Fjord in Denmark, known as Skuldelev 2, was a typical longship of the later Viking Age. It was 92 feet long and almost 15 feet wide and had thirty pairs of oars, so indicating a crew of at least sixty men. Some longships were much smaller and were useful for negotiating rivers or raiding across the Baltic, while some were much larger. *The Saga of Olaf Tryggvason* describes the great longship *Long Serpent*, which was built in Trondheim in 998, and at 160 feet in length could carry more than two hundred warriors.[8]

Magnificent though *Long Serpent* must have appeared, the account of its performance in Olaf's last great sea battle of the year 1000 against his many adversaries suggests that what it gained in accommodation it lost in maneuverability. As the opposing fleets closed in amidst a torrent of arrows and spears, Olaf commanded that *Long Serpent* be lashed between two smaller longships, probably of the Skuldelev 2 class. Olaf's aim was to create a large platform from which to resist the attackers, but boarders soon swarmed aboard the smaller vessels, clearing the decks and cutting the hawsers that bound them to *Long Serpent*.

As Olaf's leviathan came under direct attack, warriors who occupied the forecastle made the strongest resistance. Twice, boarders were repelled, but at each attempt the defenders of *Long Serpent* became fewer. At the third attempt, there were so many gaps between the men stationed along the gunwales that boarders poured through onto the decks all around the ship. The remaining crew retreated aft to protect their leader, but their fates were sealed. Olaf chose to take his chances by jumping overboard rather than face certain death. As his body was never recovered, and as news of his whereabouts continued to circulate long after his disappearance, it may be that he survived.

The other main class of longship was the cargo ship (*knörr*). These ships could carry up to sixty tons, and whole families intent on settlement could have been transported in one, lock, stock, and barrel. The recovered cargo ships Skuldelev 1 and 3 indicate, here again, the range of sizes of these ships. Skuldelev 1 was about fifty feet in length and could carry twenty-four tons, while Skuldelev 3 was about forty feet in length and carried less than five tons. Cargo ships had oar ports only in the forepart and afterpart of the ship and were almost entirely reliant on sail; they were therefore only suited to open seas or large lakes. A mere handful of men could crew a cargo ship: Skuldelev 1 required just six.

One other class of Viking longship was the *karve*. Our detailed knowledge of these ships arises from the discovery of the Gokstad and Oseberg ship burials in Norway. These exquisite vessels have been dated to the ninth century and are therefore the earliest longships that have yet been found. Both ships have similar proportions and are notable for their particularly broad hulls. It is highly unlikely that they were used on the open sea, for they were dangerously unstable. Their probable use was as royal barges or ceremonial ships. Workmanship of the highest order was employed on them, and the Oseberg ship was decorated with some of the most skillful and intricate woodcarvings that have ever been recovered from the Viking Age.

The Gokstad and Oseberg *karves* indicate most clearly the relationship between practicality and religion in Viking culture. Indeed, the longship in all its forms and functions can be regarded as symbolic of both violence and reverence. It is said, for example, that at the first launch of a longship, human blood was used to anoint the prow, and the gods were invoked to grant protection to its crew against the perils of the sea.

The dangers of the high seas were many indeed, and the sagas are full of tales of those who drowned or were blown off course. Even at best, life aboard a longship cannot have been comfortable. Every pitch and roll of the sea would have been felt, and much effort would have been taken to bale the waters that seeped in through the planking or crashed over the low sides. With no shelter aboard ship, saturation and bitter cold were among the least of the inconveniences that needed to be endured on long sea voyages. Many ships foundered. When Eirik the Red set off from Iceland in 987 with a convoy of twenty-five cargo ships and the intention of starting a settlement in southern Greenland, only fourteen of the ships completed the journey. Of the eleven that did not, some may have turned back.

Much of our knowledge of the seaworthiness, or otherwise, of Viking ships has been gained from replica voyages. In 1893, Captain Magnus Andersen sailed *Viking*, a replica of the Gokstad *karve*, from Bergen in Norway across the Atlantic to Newfoundland, and on, eventually, to Chicago. Although modified to give greater stability and buoyancy and equipped with extra sails and modern navigational equipment, *Viking* nevertheless proved the extraordinary suppleness of the longship design. Since the recovery of the Skuldelev ships in the 1960s, several replicas have tested the various speeds that types of longship could achieve, and a great deal has been learned about sail rigging and maneuverability. Replica builders have also learned that, no matter what the weather conditions, it was nearly always necessary to have at least one man baling.

But exactly how the Vikings managed to navigate the oceans without benefit of compass, sextant, or chronometer to determine latitude and longitude continues to puzzle maritime historians. A polarizing crystal, or sun stone, of the type found in Iceland might have helped, as might a sun compass of the type found in Greenland, which used a central wooden gnomon that cast a shadow across a calibrated disc. Even so, a clear view of the horizon and the sun by day and the stars by night, although highly desirable, could not be assumed, and to take readings from the sun alone necessitates an independent source of time. This would have been much more problematic.

How the Vikings plotted their course may well have been at one and the same time much simpler and much more impressive than the use of gadgets. According to a remark in the early twelfth-century Icelandic *Book of Settlements*, it is apparent that coastal navigation was much aided by oral reports.

Learned men state that from Stad in Norway it is seven days' sail west to Horn in the east of Iceland; and from Snæfellsness, where the distance is shortest, it is four days' sea west to Greenland. And it is said if one sails from Bergen due west to Hvarf in Greenland that one's course will lie some seventy or more miles south of Iceland.[9]

Advice on pilotage when land could be sighted was similarly available:

From Hernar in Norway one must sail a direct course west to Hvarf in Greenland, in which case one sails north of Shetland so that one sights land in clear weather only, then south of the Faroes so that the sea looks half-way up the mountainsides, then south of Iceland so that one gets sight of birds and whales from there.[10]

Staying in view of the coast for as long as possible, crossing open seas at the narrowest point, shrewd observations of bird and fish migrations, and the detailed reports of others—all these were the likeliest ways in which Vikings accomplished their journeys successfully. And there is more than just the possibility that our modern sense of direction has been diminished by gadgetry. Certainly the Vikings inherited thousands of years of maritime experience, and all their senses were geared toward understanding where they were. The suggestion that this understanding included a physical sense of magnetic north may not be entirely far fetched.

The warrior's way was one that demanded great courage and considerable resolve. It was also, in a sense, a duty. The Scandinavian male had long been expected to cultivate the aggressive qualities necessary for collective survival. In the

Viking Age, young men in their midteenage years were eager to prove themselves as capable warriors, and the opportunity to go on a Viking expedition was eagerly seized. Those who declined to take such opportunities were known in the Old Norse language as *heimskr*, which translates literally as "homish" but actually signifies "idiot." The Viking expansion, then, can be regarded as a belligerent exportation of a set of deeply held cultural values that was enabled by certain technological developments. The prospect of a quick profit, the search for new land, the winning of social esteem, an inherently aggressive outlook, and perhaps a contempt for Christian values may all have contributed to the warrior's way, but without the longship, that way would not have reached far beyond Scandinavia.

PART II

THE VIKING AGE

CHAPTER 3

The Conquest of England

Early Raids to Alfred the Great, 793–899

In 789, in the southern English town of Dorchester, a king's administrator by the name of Beaduheard got word that three ships of unknown origin had put to shore some twenty miles away at Portland. He gathered a few men around him and set off to instruct the strangers about their obligations to his king. Perhaps, as one source suggests, he was a little too high and mighty. Perhaps it would not have made any difference how he spoke to them, for these strangers were not the biddable kind, and, in any case, they could have had only the vaguest idea of what Beaduheard was trying to tell them. They were Norwegian Vikings, and Beaduheard did not survive their response.

None could have predicted in 789 what was to follow the murder of Beaduheard, and only in hindsight did it take on any greater significance. Over the next few years, however, there were more worrying incidents of a similar kind, sufficient to cause the powerful Mercian king, Offa, to fortify his southeast coast against pirates from the pagan north. Then, on June 8, 793, something happened that signaled the start of a new and bloody era.

The island of Lindisfarne in the far northeast of England had for centuries been a monastic center of great importance. During the seventh century, it had been home to St. Cuthbert, the renowned "Fire of the North" and the cleric who had been almost single-handedly responsible for establishing Roman Catholicism as the official church in England. Lindisfarne was a place revered across Christendom, a place of learning, consummate religious artistry, and quiet piety, and for many it was the holiest place in Britain.

The Viking attack on Lindisfarne sent tremors across the Christian world. Monks were slaughtered as they fled, others were captured and sold into slavery, and sacred relics and anything of obvious value, such as the contents of the jewelry workshop, were carted off. Much else was destroyed for the sheer wanton pleasure of it. A few monks escaped and later returned in the hope of reconstituting the community. But one Viking attack usually meant that another would follow. Eventually, it was deemed prudent to seek a safe resting place for the apparently incorrupt remains of the blessed Cuthbert and the one priceless treasure that the Vikings, in their ignorance, would scarcely have appreciated—the beautifully illuminated Lindisfarne Bible. With little chance of continuing a meditative life while Viking marauders infested the seas, Lindisfarne was all but abandoned and would not be recolonized fully for three hundred years. Alcuin, the most learned Englishman of the age and secretary to the Holy Roman emperor, Charlemagne, at Aachen in Francia, articulated the shock that all felt after the sacrilege at Lindisfarne.

We and our forefathers have now lived in this fair land for nearly three hundred and fifty years, and never before has such an atrocity been seen in Britain as we have now suffered at the hands of a pagan people. Such a voyage was not thought possible. The church of St. Cuthbert is spattered with the blood of the priests of God, stripped of all its furnishings, exposed to the plundering of pagans—a place more sacred than any in Britain.[1]

For Alcuin, however, this was not only a desecration by pagan savages but also a divine punishment, a consequence of moral degeneration in Northumbria. Like the compilers of the *Anglo-Saxon Chronicle* writing a hundred years later, Alcuin believed that the enormity at Lindisfarne had been heralded in portents during previous months. Immense flashes of lightning, whirlwinds, great famine, dragons flying through the air, and a rain of blood over the minster at York—all these presaged divine retribution.

The riches of Anglo-Saxon England that the Vikings began to eye greedily in the late eighth century were relatively easy pickings. Partly enabling aggressive intrusion was the fact that England was not a unified realm. The four main kingdoms—Northumbria spanning the north, Mercia covering the midlands, East Anglia to the east, and Wessex ranging across most of the south—were often at odds with each other. The population—probably little more than a million—largely comprised peasant farmers clustered in small hamlets, remote even from each other. The commercial centers, the *wics*, and the ports were typically poorly defended places, and the same was true of the monasteries, many of which were deliberately located in remoter regions, often near the coast. Scandinavian traders had for decades been active in Northumbria, and information that England was vulnerable to attack from the sea rapidly circulated among more predatory seafarers. As Alcuin explicitly acknowledged, no such attack from the pagan north had ever been thought likely or even possible. The kingdoms of England were complacent.

While the Vikings would have apprehended nothing of the theological alarm that their attack on Lindisfarne triggered, they quickly apprehended the ease with which they could cross the North Atlantic and head down into the Irish and North Seas. Their staging posts were the secluded harbors of the Orkney and Shetland Isles off the northeast tip of Scotland, and the Hebridean archipelago in the Irish Sea. From these lairs, slaves could be mustered, booty stashed, and further raids planned. By the end of the first quarter of the ninth century, as the *Annals of Ulster* reported with increasing monotony, Vikings were despoiling the holy places on a yearly basis.

Certain particularly ripe targets were ransacked time and time again. St. Columba, the monastic center of the Celtic church on the island of Iona off the west coast of Scotland, was raided in 795, 802, and 806, when, in this last instant, sixty monks were put to death. So wearied were the monks that, in 814, most relocated to Kells in Ireland, leaving only a few behind who readied themselves for martyrdom. In 825, when Vikings came looking for the sacred shrine of St. Columba, martyrdom was achieved by some, including Prior Blathmacc mac Flaind, who was tortured to death for refusing to betray the shrine's whereabouts. As one Irish monk lamented, bad weather was the only guarantee of a peaceful night:

> Bitter is the wind tonight,
> It tosses the white-waved sea,
> I do not fear the coursing of the great sea
> By the fierce warriors from Norway.[2]

Ireland caught much of the brunt of these early attacks. Sparsely populated and torn by tribal rivalries, Ireland was perfectly disposed for the Viking policy of hit and run. Internal chaos was easily exploited, and, in time, parcels of land on the east coast were seized and fortified. During the late 830s, these became the *longphorts*, Viking-owned and controlled harbors and commercial centers. Chief among the *longphorts* was Dublin, and it was from there that ambitious Vikings would seek to extend their power across Scotland and northern England for the next 120 years.

While the situation around the coastal fringes of northern Britain and in Ireland was shifting from raids to colonization, southern England remained relatively unaffected until the 830s. Danish Vikings had almost exclusively targeted Francia up until 835. Then, suddenly, the situation changed. What had been sporadic attacks across northern Francia and down the western littoral saw a dramatic escalation as Vikings began to act more concertedly and in much greater numbers. With Norwegian Vikings growing increasingly dominant in the Celtic west, England found itself at the center of the two main theaters of Viking activity. The English Channel soon became crowded with Danish longships heading for England's southeast coastline.

In 835, the Isle of Sheppey on the Thames estuary became a launching pad for Vikings plundering across Kent. Then, a year later, approximately thirty longships, probably of Norwegian origin, were reported to have attacked Carhampton in the West Country, perhaps hoping to ally themselves with the rebellious Cornish, who resented the rule of Wessex kings. But it was the threat in the east of the country, from the Danes, that proved most dangerous. For the next fourteen years, Danish Vikings probed English defenses. Win or lose, they were undeterred, and in 850, for the first time, a large army settled itself into winter quarters on the Isle of Thanet off the eastern tip of Kent.

In the *Chronicle* entry for the following year, the writers probably exaggerated when they claimed that 350 longships had entered the River Thames, but there can be little doubt that this assault was on a scale previously unknown. On the way to London, the Viking army stormed Canterbury, the principal city of Kent and England's oldest religious center, and at London, they forced the Mercian king and his army into flight. Emboldened, they then moved south into Surrey. There, however, a Wessex army was ready for them and "made the greatest slaughter of a heathen raiding army that we have heard tell of up to this present day."[3] In the same year, Wessex ships took on the Vikings at sea, capturing nine longships and driving off the rest. Wessex resistance and its high level of military organization was a good sign for the future, but at the time the Vikings were undaunted.

During the course of the next decade, the inhabitants of Kent became so oppressed by Viking raiders that by 865 they preferred to pay them to go away rather than suffer the inevitable ruination of property and the attendant loss of life. It was an ineffective strategy, for the Vikings simply accepted the bribe and then went about business as usual. It was, perhaps, the same army that had extorted "Danegeld," from the burghers of Kent that moved north to East Anglia, to form part of the Danish Great Army led by the notorious Ragnarssons. Perhaps, too, the move north was prompted by the need for a firmer footing.

As discussed in the introduction, the taking of York in 866 was a pivotal moment in England's Viking Age. The seven-year campaign that followed was astonishingly successful for the Great Army, and with the kingdoms of Northumbria, East Anglia, and Mercia all under direct Viking control by 873, only the southern kingdom of Wessex remained sovereign.

The newly crowned Æthelred, king of Wessex, and his younger brother Alfred had been obliged to stand by helpless after the siege of Nottingham in 867, when their brother-in-law, Burgred, king of Mercia, had conceded payment and, it would seem, much of his authority to the Ragnarssons. Then, in 871, Halfdan Ragnarsson moved the Great Army south to Reading in Berkshire, with the sole intention of destroying the power of Wessex. A series of battles was fought. Several Danish leaders were slain in the process, and the *Chronicle* reports that at the Battle of Ashdown, many thousands of Vikings died. A conspicuous Danish victory followed Ashdown, and then something like stalemate at a place recorded as Meretun but otherwise unknown. Though not beaten, the Vikings had had enough, as surely had the Wessex men. A truce was agreed, and the Vikings withdrew into Mercia. For the time being, Wessex was safe, but in the same year, tragedy struck when King Æthelred died. The Wessex crown now fell to the young Alfred. It was a momentous succession, for it is sometimes the case that the future history of a nation depends wholly on the deeds and character of just one person. Such was the case with Alfred of Wessex.

After the truce of 871, the Great Army once more turned its attention to Mercia. The *Chronicle* reports that the Vikings first took winter quarters at London and in the following year moved north and did likewise in Lindsey, south of the River Humber. On both occasions, we are told, "the Mercians made peace with the raiding-army,"[4] although this was more than likely a euphemism for fearful and costly compliance. After the third winter camp at Repton and the dismissal of the Mercian king, Burgred, the Great Army divided. Halfdan returned to the north, and by 875 he was back in York, dividing up Northumbria among his men. While the Vikings in Northumbria were "ploughing and providing for themselves,"[5] the other half of the army moved south to the Mercian town of Cambridge. Leading the army was Guthrum, the Viking king of East Anglia since the martyrdom of King Edmund in 869. Alfred was clearly already dealing with a Viking threat off his coastline, and while the Viking army was squatting ominously in Cambridge, Alfred took to the sea and captured a Viking longship and saw off six others. Then, in an audacious and what would appear to be a wholly unexpected move, Guthrum marched his army right into the heart of Alfred's kingdom and took the fortified town of Wareham on the south coast.

Alfred now made his first big mistake. Believing that he could buy himself out of trouble, money was handed over and hostages were exchanged, and when Guthrum swore great oaths, declaring that he would leave Wessex without further ado, he was believed. It was all a sham, for no sooner had the truce been agreed than Guthrum executed the hostages Alfred had delivered to him and marched his army sixty miles west to another of Alfred's fortresses at Exeter. Alfred laid siege but could not dislodge them. Another truce was agreed, and, expedient though it was to do so, Alfred can have set little store in Guthrum's renewed promises of peace. This time, however, the Viking army did actually leave Wessex and for a while satisfied itself by rampaging around southwestern Mercia.

At the Christmastime of 877, Alfred and his entourage settled on his royal estate at Chippenham. Little in the way of trouble can have been expected, but as the year turned and the religious festivities came to a close, Guthrum returned. Completely taken off guard, Alfred fled for his life. Guthrum pressed on deeper into Wessex, laying waste to everything in his path. Alfred's army was dispersed, and his subjects were driven from their land. Not knowing whether their king still lived, many chose to submit to Guthrum's authority. Alfred reached his lowest ebb. He and a handful of retainers took refuge in the marshlands of Somerset. For the winter and spring, Alfred could do little but live off the land and launch the occasional guerrilla raid against passing Viking foot soldiers and Christian collaborators. Legend has it that during this period, he took refuge with a swineherd whose wife instructed him to look after the oven where her cakes were baking, but in his distracted state, he let the cakes to burn. True or not, it is nevertheless an apt metaphor for Alfred's lack of vigilance.

Yet, although Wessex may have appeared beaten, much of its network of loyalties and obligations was still intact. All was not quite lost, and Alfred was determined that what few resources he had left should be put to good use. His gradual and quite remarkable recovery spawned extravagant explanations. One story tells how Alfred had a vision of St. Cuthbert who advised him how to beat Guthrum, and another tells how Alfred disguised himself as a wandering minstrel and entered into the enemy encampment and eavesdropped on their plans. In any case, from his Somerset hideaway, Alfred was soon sending out word that he intended to raise an army. Those who could carry a weapon should meet with him that Easter at Ecgberht's Stone, a secluded spot in the Forest of Selwood that commemorated Alfred's grandfather, the founder of the might of Wessex. Thousands rallied to Alfred's standard.

Meanwhile, not everything had been going the way of the invaders. In the same winter that Alfred was made fugitive, Ubba Ragnarsson, the last surviving brother of the trio that took York in 866, met his death along with eight hundred of his men at the hands of a Devon army. Somewhat ominously for the Vikings, their sacred raven banner was seized in the encounter. Now it was Guthrum's turn to be unvigilant. While he was comfortably ensconced at Chippenham, the main force of his army was thirty miles to the south at Edington.

Gathering support as he went, Alfred marched his followers to Edington, where they confronted Guthrum's Vikings. The English victory was decisive. Remnants of the Viking army fled to Chippenham, where for fourteen days Alfred laid siege. Eventually worn down by "hunger, cold and fear, and in the end by despair,"[6] Guthrum capitulated, and this time Alfred was of no mind to make truces or offer settlement or exchange hostages or any such thing in order to persuade Guthrum to leave. This time he would have from Guthrum a deeper understanding of the meaning of a promise. The pagan would become a Christian, and Alfred himself would act as godfather. At Aller, near Alfred's Somerset hideout, and a week later at Wedmore, a treaty was concluded, during which Guthrum donned his white baptismal robes and readily submitted to Alfred's impressive war god. A year later, back in his East Anglian kingdom, Guthrum was pleased to issue coins inscribed with the name Athelstan, his baptismal name.

For the next ten years of Alfred's rule, he set about making sure that no Viking army would ever again threaten his sovereignty. Across the Wessex territories, he established more than thirty permanently manned fortifications known as the *burhs*. As a result, Alfred could raise over twenty-seven thousand men for garrison duty alone. He also advanced the cause of a united England. Ties with West, or English, Mercia, which still eluded dominance by the Vikings, were strengthened when Alfred married off his daughter Æthelflæd to the region's leading ealdorman, a certain Æthelred. It was a liaison that would become critical after Alfred's death. More than this, when Alfred was forced to seize London because Guthrum momentarily forgot his oaths, Alfred was acknowledged as the overlord of all the English who were not under Danish subjection. Under Alfred, the idea of a free English people bound by law and culture first became a reality, and although the Vikings still held a firm grip on much of the country, the notion of a politically united England emerged as a credible ideal.

When, in 892, another wave of Vikings set on conquest and colonization crossed the English Channel from Francia, Alfred was well prepared. By his side was his son Edward, a prince very much in his father's mold. Leading the Second Great Army of Vikings was the notorious Hastein, the scourge of the Franks. For three years, Alfred and Edward harassed and disrupted Hastein's army. The Vikings were prevented from coming together in large assembly; a scorched-earth policy sent them on wide detours through Danish-held East Mercia and East Anglia to gather provisions or find a way back to their southeastern encampments; and when they left their encampments to go raiding, they returned to find their long-ships scuttled, their women and children taken captive, and their stolen goods reclaimed. By 895, Alfred calculated that a single payment would send Hastein and company packing. This time, he was right.

For the remaining four years of Alfred's life, his military energies were given over to building up his navy. Few Vikings dared threaten his Wessex borders or coastline. One raiding party of six longships that did encountered an Alfred who was in no mood to parley. Only one ship escaped, and those Vikings who survived the wreckage of the other five were taken back to Alfred's seat of government at Winchester and hanged.

Alfred died on October 26, 899. He had ruled for twenty-eight years. His military achievements alone would have assured Alfred a notable place in English history, but there was much more to his reign than this.

Alfred's formidable efforts in the areas of literature and scholarship, as a translator of classical and religious texts; his determination to revive religious learning and to introduce a program of education for all the nobility; and his establishment of unified principles of English law created a cultural strength in England that would outlive its conquest by Viking kings in the early eleventh century and by the French in 1066. Late medieval English kings honored him as "the Great," but to the Anglo-Saxons, he was a more accessible figure, and they knew him as "*Englene hirde, englene deorling*"—"England's shepherd, England's darling." As his contemporaries and successors knew quite well, without Alfred of Wessex, there would not have been an England left to defend.

Wessex versus the Kingdom of York, 899–954

Tenth-century York—Jorvik, as it was known in the Norse tongue—was a boomtown. The rivers Ouse and Foss, which wound through the walled city and joined to flow southeast into the River Humber and so out into the North Sea, were main arterial highways for Viking Age traffic. Longships came and went carrying merchandise from all over the Viking world: spices, silks, and precious stones from the Mediterranean and the Middle East; furs, ivory, and amber from Scandinavia; and human cargo from the Dublin slave markets and elsewhere. York was a powerhouse of industry where Viking merchants could refit their ships and purchase a vast array of manufactured goods. In its crowded and noisome streets, Northumbrians and Scandinavians, Christians and pagans, mingled and gradually merged into a single cultural identity.

Within fifty years of the taking of York, the city had become home to a population of over ten thousand people, with their own church authority, their own traditions of kingship, and their own vibrant economy. They had little time for ambitious Wessex kings, and all the time in the world for enterprise and profit. Yet, after the death of Alfred, it was at York that the battle for the domination of England became focused, for Alfred's ambition to unite England was inherited without any dilution by all of his successors.

When Alfred's son, Edward, succeeded him in 899, he immediately ran into a difficulty. It came in the form of Æthelwold, the son of Alfred's brother, the late King Æthelred. Æthelwold felt that he, not Edward, should be king of Wessex, and he showed his displeasure by seizing a royal manor and a fortress. When Edward went to rebuke him, Æthelwold fled from Wessex to join the Vikings in York. Not unnaturally, the Vikings were delighted and promptly elected him king. Matters came to a head when Edward's army of Kent and Wessex regulars met Æthelwold's Viking army in the fens of East Anglia. Chaos ensued. The two main elements of Edward's army lost contact with each other, and the Vikings wreaked havoc among the confused English. But this did Æthelwold no good, as it was his misfortune to be killed. Both sides withdrew.

With dynastic controversies out of the way, Edward now concentrated on the main matter at hand: the recovery of English land from the Danes. The Æthelwold affair had led Edward to make a treaty with the East Anglians and the Northumbrians, leaving only Mercia as contested ground. Chances of the immediate recovery of Danish-held East Mercia were slight, for the so-called Five Boroughs of Lincoln, Nottingham, Derby, Leicester, and Stamford were powerful Viking bulwarks.

Then, in 909, Edward decided to provoke the situation by launching a lightning attack through East Mercia and across the Northumbrian border. The following year, the Vikings retaliated with an attack on West Mercia. This was probably just what Edward wanted. The Vikings were routed at Tettenhall near the Welsh border, and as a result Edward's hand was considerably strengthened. When ealdorman Æthelred of West Mercia died the following year, Edward gained, by proxy, even greater authority, for Æthelflæd, the "Lady of the Mercians," took control of her late husband's territory. A son and a daughter of Alfred were now the greatest powers among the English. Their first task was to accomplish in West Mercia what their father had accomplished in Wessex and make it impregnable.

By 917, Edward and Æthelflæd were ready to put their war plan into operation. All that was needed was the right moment, and the Vikings inevitably supplied it when they launched yet another ill-judged attack. While Vikings hurled themselves to little effect at the new *burh* fortifications of West Mercia, Æthelflæd moved swiftly and took two of the Five Boroughs. The English advance looked unstoppable as Edward cowed the Vikings of East Anglia and brought two more of the boroughs under his control. Then, as the fight for England reached a tipping point, Æthelflæd suddenly died.

Edward had no choice but to hurry back to West Mercia and assert his kingship, fearful that the West Mercians would elect Æthelflæd's daughter and so disdain his authority. When he returned to East Mercia, he was just able to over-run the fifth borough before his momentum was spent. The Northumbrian Kingdom of York still lay beyond his reach. Edward's achievement was nevertheless considerable, for now "all the people who had settled in Mercia, both Danish and English, turned to him."[7] Viking England had been reduced to exactly what it was when the Ragnarssons first took York in 866. Given the network of fortifications across Mercia and the military readiness of the Wessex kings, there was far less likelihood of Viking leaders once again making gains of the magnitude of those made by the Danish Great Army. Such inhibitions, however, did not stop them from trying.

A clear, although rarely coordinated, aim of the Vikings had always been the establishment of a York–Dublin axis from which they could exert their power southward. After the Vikings were evicted from Dublin in 902, there was obvi-ously no prospect of progress in this regard, but when they returned to Dublin in 917, the York–Dublin axis was immedi-ately put at the top of the agenda. A substantial settlement of chiefly Norwegian Vikings in the northwest of England and in the southwest of Scotland had established something of a land bridge between Vikings in Ireland and the Kingdom of

York. Soon, there were three grandsons of Ivar the Boneless contending not only for Dublin but also for York: Ragnald, Sihtric, and Guthfrith. It was the eldest of these, Ragnald, who assumed the kingship of York in 919.

Ragnald was astute enough to realize that at that moment in time Edward was unassailable. Sharing Ragnald's conclusion were the Scots, whose feelings of ill will toward the English were equally deep seated. For the time being, it was judicious for all concerned to acknowledge Edward as "father and lord," but this most certainly did not mean that they were prepared to surrender their autonomy. For the enemies of the English, it was a time for consolidation.

Any immediate threat from the Kingdom of York was reduced in 920 when Ragnald died, but it was soon revived when his brother Sihtric, known also as "the Squinter," relocated to York from Dublin. Four years later, Edward also died, and his son and successor, the talented and sophisticated Athelstan, decided to try and draw York into the Wessex ambit by marrying his daughter to Sihtric on the condition that he convert. But Sihtric failed to grasp the significance of a Christian marriage and resumed his pagan ways within a year of the nuptials. His wife, it is said, took the veil.

More confusion followed when Sihtric died and the third brother, Guthfrith, hurried over from Dublin to take his place. Athelstan now appreciated that his hopes for an accommodation with Dublin warlords at York was a lost cause and decided on the military option. In 927, he entered York and forcibly evicted Guthfrith. For the next ten years, Athelstan could be spoken of as the first king of all the English, and although his hold over northern Britain was precarious, his authority went largely unchallenged. But back in Dublin, resentments ran deep, in particular with Guthfrith's son, Olaf, who regarded York as part and parcel of his patrimony. Olaf began to make plans. A major showdown was in the offing.

Olaf Guthfrithsson's scheme was to forge an alliance between all the northern powers. Hiberno-Norsemen, Anglo-Scandinavians, Scots, Celtic Britons from Strathclyde, and Vikings of every kind would all be brought together into a coalition against the power of the Wessex king. In 937, in what was remembered as one of the bloodiest battles that was ever fought in Anglo-Saxon England, Olaf and his allies took to the field against Athelstan at a place called Brunanburh in northern England. Much of what we know about the Battle of Brunanburh is derived from a commemorative and propagandizing Old English poem, seventy lines of which are recorded in the *Anglo-Saxon Chronicle*. Praise is heaped on the English elite cavalry and on the tactical brilliance and raw courage of Athelstan and his sixteen-year-old brother Edmund, who "won themselves eternal glory / In battle with the edges of their swords."[8] Aiding Athelstan, perhaps to the surprise of his foes, were a number of Viking mercenaries who saw it as more honorable to side with a bona fide English king than with a Dublin pretender.

The battle raged from dawn until dusk, and the casualties on both sides numbered in the thousands. Olaf 's coalition army was cut to pieces, and among the notable coalition dead were the son of King Constantine II of Scotland, five lesser Viking kings, and seven Viking *jarls* (earls). Olaf, himself, barely escaped with his life. The poem relishes his humiliation:

There the Norsemen's chief
Was put to flight, and driven by dire need

With small retinue to seek his ship.

The ship pressed out to sea, the king departed

Onto the yellow flood and saved his life.[9]

Yet Brunanburh was not as significant as Athelstan's comprehensive victory over his northern enemies might suggest. Two years later, Athelstan was dead, and with scarcely a pause for breath, Olaf Guthfrithsson was back in York. Within a year, he had recaptured the Five Boroughs. Edmund, Athelstan's successor, seemed unable to mount a response, and it would not be until after Olaf's death in 941 that Edmund was finally able recover what had been lost.

The final chapter in the story of York is as farcical as it is chaotic. Two more Dublin warlords—Olaf Sandal, the son of Sihtric, and Ragnald, the brother of Olaf Guthfrithsson—fell into open rivalry over the vacancy at York. In 946, Edmund was moved to intervene and sent both contenders back whence they came, although in the case of Olaf Sandal, this proved to be only a temporary deportation. Then, in 948, after Edmund's death, another Viking added his name to the cast list. This claimant was neither from Dublin nor a descendant of Ivar the Boneless but a pagan Norwegian king in exile, the aptly named Eirik Bloodaxe.

If, as was claimed in one Icelandic saga, Eirik had been promised York by Athelstan in order that the warlike Norwegian should act as a buffer against the Scots, then it was an uncharacteristically bad decision by the Wessex king. But whatever might have been the reason behind Eirik's arrival in England, the consequence was that, for the next six years, York became the scene of a giddy game of musical thrones.

It was during this period that the separatist agenda that had long united the Anglo-Scandinavian communities of the Kingdom of York began to look less and less attractive to them. First they turned out Eirik and restored Olaf, and then they turned out Olaf and restored Eirik. In the end, neither alternative appealed. In 954, Eirik was deposed a second time, and this time the Northumbrians made quite sure he would not be coming back. As Eirik and his retinue headed northwest toward Scotland, expecting to set sail for the Orkney Isles, a gang of assassins emerged from the roadside "at a certain lonely place called Stainmore" and slaughtered every one of them.[10]

The Viking tenancy of York was in this way ended, and the dream of a united England became a firm reality. Whatever territorial disputes were to follow on from this, they would not be piecemeal battles over petty kingdoms but wars over a nation.

Wars of Conquest, 980–1066

Framed among the serpentine scrolls on a tenth-century grave slab that now rests in the vaults of York Minster is a depiction of Sigurd, the greatest hero of Scandinavian legend, slaying the wicked dragon Fafnir. Yet this ornamentation does not honor a deceased Viking pagan but a deceased Anglo-Scandinavian Christian. In the churchyard of the village of Gosforth, in the northwest of England, a fourteen-foot-high sandstone cross shows several intricately carved scenes from the twilight of the Norse gods at Ragnarok. On one face, the apocalyptic wolf Fenrir, mouth agape, descends on Odin. Beneath it is Christ on the cross, and beneath him is the Virgin Mary, pigtailed and wearing a long smock in the manner of a Valkyrie. Mary appears to stand on the back of two intertwined monsters snarling into each other's faces.

Across the Viking settlements in the north of England, numerous such artifacts can be found. In some cases, explicitly Christian images have been defaced and carved over with scenes from Norse myth and legend. In the century following the Viking colonization of northern England, a hybrid culture developed. Christian conversion had slowly taken place, but the theological stock in trade of Christian iconography became merged with the traditions of pagan Scandinavia. And the church, ever ready to compromise in order to embrace new converts, absorbed into its repertoire of powerful images many expressions that at one time it had regarded as abominable.

The extent to which Scandinavian settlement transformed the north is, by one measure, indicated in the place-names that still figure on the way markers of northern lanes and byways. Almost forty percent of the names of towns and villages that were once in the Viking Kingdom of York contain elements from the Old Norse language, most evidently in the place-name endings of *-by* and *-thorpe*, which indicated the quality of the land. In many other cases, existing Anglo-Saxon settlements were simply overrun by Viking colonists. In place-names such as Grimston, the Viking leader Grim had added his name to the Old English settlement marker *-tun*. Colonization did not always involve hiving off a few acres of undeveloped land; just as often it took the form of an occupation of existing settlements, a dispossession.

In the united England finally achieved by Wessex kings in 954, there were profound cultural differences. For peace and unity to hold, this had to be recognized. When Edgar, the son of Edmund and foster son of Athelstan, came to rule England in 959, he wisely decided that the areas of his realm that were indelibly printed with Viking mores and traditions should be allowed a degree of autonomy in their customs and practices.

> It is my will that there should be in force among the Danes such good laws as they best decide on, and I have ever allowed this and will allow it as long as my life lasts, because of your loyalty which you have always shown me.[11]

Thus, the region known as the Danelaw received royal sanction. Yet there was one important proviso.

> Nevertheless, this measure is to be common to all the nation, whether Englishmen, Danes or Britons, in every province of my dominion, to the end that the poor man and rich may possess what they rightly acquire.[12]

The Danes were acknowledged as a special case, but this should not be allowed to jeopardize the rights of any other Englishman.

While Edgar was setting the Danes in order in England, significant problems were looming in their Scandinavian homelands. Trade with the Arab caliphate had been a chief source of income for Viking kings and warlords since the late ninth century. Vast quantities of silver, extracted from Arab silver mines and paid in coin to Viking merchants and adventurers, had not only underpinned commercial and piratical activities, but had also financed the struggles of kings seeking to achieve national unity in the three main Scandinavian countries.

In and around the early 970s, these silver mines were exhausted, and, as a consequence, trade with the Arabs all but ceased. Coupled with this, Viking efforts to control Ireland suffered an irreversible setback in 980, when Olaf Sandal squandered Viking power in a "red slaughter" at the Battle of Tara. After this, Vikings in Ireland became little more than pawns in a deadly game of internal Irish power politics, which culminated in 1014 in the calamitous Battle of Clontarf. Nor was there any further possibility of exploiting Francia, which was by this time stabilized and, in any case, largely defended by one-time Vikings who had turned respectable. Determined to find new sources of income, Scandinavian warlords yet again looked toward England.

Unbeknownst to the Viking leaders of England's second Viking Age, the pluck and, it should be admitted, the luck of the Wessex kings had run out. In 979, Æthelred, the second son of Edgar, came to the throne. In later years, Anglo-Saxon historians would pun on his Christian name meaning "wise counsel" and append to it *un-raed*, meaning "badly counseled." It is a good joke in the vernacular, but Æthelred is probably better remembered, and not inappropriately so, as Æthelred the Unready.

During the 980s, a rash of Viking raids befell southern England. As had been the case 150 years previously, it once again looked as though the Vikings were probing English defenses, as if unsure what the possibilities might be. By end of the decade, they seemed to have arrived at a conclusion. Not only was there a great deal of booty to be had, but, more than this, in time and with sufficient numbers, conquest was possible. The question was, what could Æthelred do to stop it?

Northey Island is little more than a hundred yards from the Essex town of Maldon. At low tide, a causeway connects Northey to the mainland. In 991, a fleet of ninety-three long-ships set about raiding around the southeast coast and eventually put to land on Northey. Ealdorman Byrhtnoth of Essex rallied his men to defend the causeway. The Anglo-Saxon poem "The Battle of Maldon"[13] tells how the heathen "wolves of war" demanded tribute, and how Byrhtnoth scorned their request but then, somewhat strangely, offered them safe passage across the causeway so they could engage with his army. Byrhtnoth and his men were duly annihilated. In the absence of anything to celebrate militarily, the poem does its best to salute the bravery of those English who did not desert. Yet what the poem really acknowledges is a national crisis.

Captaining the Viking fleet at Maldon was a certain Olaf Tryggvason, an aspirant for the throne of Norway. It is quite possible that he had with him the current King of Denmark, Svein Forkbeard. Under this leadership, thousands of Vikings were now on the loose not far north of London. King Æthelred took counsel and decided that his best policy was to bribe them to go away. Ten thousand pounds of silver were handed over, and the Vikings departed. Paying "Danegeld" was not Æthelred's idea in the first instant, but it was one that he never abandoned.

Three years later, Olaf and his army returned, this time to threaten London. Æthelred yet again dug into the national coffers and offered Olaf sixteen thousand pounds of silver to leave, on the condition that he become a Christian and promise never again to trouble English shores. Olaf readily agreed and sailed back to Norway where he could now buy the support he needed to become king.

The folly of Æthelred's policy was soon apparent to all but him as reports of Olaf 's bargains circulated among Viking contemporaries. In the final years of the tenth century, southern England, the West Country, and Wales were crawling with Vikings, all of them keen to cause sufficient trouble to warrant Æthelred's largesse. Æthelred realized that matters could not go on like this and issued a decree to the effect that on St. Brice's Day, November 13, 1002, "all the Danes who had sprung up in this island, sprouting like weeds among the wheat, were to be destroyed by a most just extermination."[14] This ethnic cleansing was politically inept, wholly miscalculated, and largely bungled. Worse still, it had one consequence that would ultimately lead to Æthelred's downfall. On St. Brice's Day in Oxford, men, women, and children of Danish origin fled to St. Frideswides' Minster to take sanctuary. The mob surrounded the minster and set it alight. Among those who were burned alive were the sister and brother-in-law of the Danish king Svein Forkbeard. Now Æthelred had a blood feud on his hands.

Svein Forkbeard's twelve-year war against Æthelred's England was an undisguised campaign of conquest. During this time, the southern counties of England were completely overrun, treachery and confusion were rife among the English aristocracy—Æthelred even managed to destroy his own navy when it was seized by defectors—the archbishop of Canterbury was murdered by drunken Vikings, and Æthelred doled out a further 110,000 pounds of silver to his country's tormentors.

By 1013, no one in England was in any doubt about what the outcome was going to be. Æthelred fled with his wife, Emma, to her royal kin in Normandy, and Svein was promptly acknowledged as the new king-in-waiting of all England. It is noticeable that during the years of strife, no Viking force sought to trouble the Scandophile north, and there is no record of the north seeking to intervene on behalf of their English king.

Svein's claim on the English throne was undisputed, but before he could be crowned, he died. The Viking army in the field elected his son, Cnut, and doubtless assumed that what the father had won the son would inherit, but the English nobility saw a slim chance of recovery and declined to accept him. Cnut withdrew to Denmark to equip himself for the task ahead, and in 1015 he returned to England with a vast fleet. By this time, Æthelred was too ill to take issue with him, and the following year he would die "after great toil and difficulties in life," as the *Chronicle* considerately observed.[15]

It fell to Edmund Ironside, son of Æthelred the Unready, to take on Cnut's formidable invasion force. Edmund, as his appellation suggests, had something about him of the fighting spirit of Wessex kings of old, but such was the disarray caused by his father's incompetence that he could not command a loyal following. During the course of 1016, Edmund ably fought against Cnut and in due course might have won were it not for the treachery of a certain English general during the final encounter at Ashingdon, north of the Thames estuary. Defeated and badly injured, Edmund was obliged to accept the rule of Wessex as his only entitlement, while Cnut would rule all else. When, a few weeks later, Edmund's wounds proved fatal, Cnut, son of Svein, became the unopposed king of the entire country. Two years on from his coronation, Denmark and large slices of Norway and Sweden were added to Cnut's North Sea empire.

The twelfth-century historian Henry of Huntingdon told how Cnut once took his throne to the seashore and sat there with waves lapping around him, wildly commanding the tide to turn. In modern times, the inference often drawn from this is that Cnut was a ridiculous megalomaniac. In actuality, the purpose of Henry's story was to indicate that the opposite was true. Cnut knew perfectly well that to rule over England he needed to adapt to, and absorb, the traditions of Anglo-Saxon Christian kingship. He needed to show respect and humility without at the same time showing weakness. Yet none in England had ever experienced a king who wielded such power and majesty, and much was expected of him. As Henry pointed out, Cnut's defiance of the tide was a rather dramatic demonstration of the limits of his power, not the extent of it.

Cnut's eighteen-year reign was characterized by radical internal reforms and a firm determination to consolidate his power abroad. When he issued a public proclamation reassuring his people that no Viking would ever again threaten English shores, some may have found a dark irony in the king's promise. Nevertheless, it is apparent that Cnut's time was one of peace and progress for the English. Æthelred's slovenly aristocracy was replaced by men who shared Cnut's vision of Anglo-Danish unity; the law was codified and reaffirmed according to the principles of unity among diversity that Edgar had established; and a great deal of money was invested in revitalizing monastic life, much of this by way of making public reparation for the damage done by Cnut's forebears.

Cnut astutely married his daughter to the son of the German emperor, and he underscored his own legitimacy by marrying

Emma, Æthelred's widow. However, his lifelong attachment to his Northampton concubine, Ælfgifu, and to the son she delivered him, led to considerable dynastic confusion after his death in 1035, for among the claimants to the throne were not only his illegitimate son but also his sons by Emma as well as Emma's sons by Æthelred.

It took seven years of ferocious dynastic rivalry to settle the succession issue. Between times, Cnut's empire in Scandinavia was lost, and true power in England shifted away from the king and toward the ruthlessly ambitious Earl Godwin of Wessex, a onetime pirate who had been raised to prominence by Cnut. When Edward, son of Æthelred, became king in 1042, it was Godwin who really held the reins of power. Godwin's designs on the throne were flagrant, and his political luster acquired a tinge of royal blue when he obliged Edward to marry his daughter, Edith. Edward gradually withdrew into a private world of piety and prayer, so gaining the title Edward the Confessor. When Edward died childless in January 1066, the council of nobles, the witan, disregarded all other claims to succeed him and set the crown on the head of Godwin's powerful, soldierly son, Harold. It was to be a brief but memorable reign.

Exactly how William the Bastard, Duke of Normandy, latest in line of a dynasty founded by Vikings in the early tenth century, came to think he was entitled to rule England is something of a mystery. One theory is that it was Harold Godwinson himself who had rashly promised overlordship to William during an unintended visit to William's court in 1065. Another theory is that it was Edward the Confessor—more French in his outlook than English—who had anointed William his successor, much in the manner of a dead hand designed to frustrate Earl Godwin. Whichever the case, William's face was set against Harold. He was astute enough to ensure that he had the backing of Pope Alexander II for the enterprise he was planning.

If the origins of Duke William's claim are one mystery, another one is whatever it was that encouraged Harald Hard-Ruler, king of Norway, to believe that he too had a right to succeed Edward the Confessor. Perhaps, as may well have been the case, a deal involving the English throne had been struck thirty years previously between his nephew, Magnus, and Harthacnut, son of Cnut, during Harthacnut's messy reigns over Denmark and England. And perhaps that was all that the likes of Harald Hard-Ruler needed as an excuse. This being so, the legitimacy of Harald's claim was at least as obscure as William's. But, there again, the succession of Harold Godwinson was hardly uncontroversial.

Two things became clear as 1066 progressed: the first was that King Harold expected trouble from Duke William and believed that it would arrive very soon; the second was that he had not the faintest idea that trouble was brewing up north. Harald Hard-Ruler was the last of the Viking warlords. His career had taken him down through Russia and on into Byzantium, where he had given service to four Greek emperors and, in the process, had amassed a fortune and attracted the epithet "the Thunderbolt of the North." Harald's plan to conquer England was the same as the one hatched by the Ragnarsson's exactly two hundred years earlier. His initial target was York.

There is no eyewitness account of what exactly took place during the battles that followed at York. The *Anglo-Saxon Chronicle* gives certain credible details in two manuscripts, and there is a much longer and more colorful account of the conflict in Snorri Sturluson's saga of Harald Hard-Ruler. In this latter case, some caution with respect to battle tactics needs to be exercised, given that it was written over a century and a half later. Mention, for example, of the English forces gaining the upper hand through the use of cavalry is probably anachronistic and may say more about Snorri's knowledge of battles during the Crusades than about his knowledge of military conflict in Anglo-Saxon England. Yet there is no discrepancy between English and Scandinavian sources concerning the final outcome of Harald's war of conquest.

According to Snorri's saga, in the early autumn of 1066, in company with Harold Godwinson's disaffected brother Tostig, Harald Hard-Ruler led his longships to the northeast coast of England, burned down the coastal town of Scarborough, and headed for York with an army reckoned to have been nine thousand strong. At Fulford, outside of York, he overcame the stalwart resistance of the Northumbrian earls and established his camp at Stamford Bridge. There, he decided to rest while arrangements were made for him to enter York in such a manner as would befit a conquering Norwegian king.

Meanwhile, in the south, Harold Godwinson was scanning the English Channel and anticipating the fleet of Duke William. When news reached him of Harald Hard-Ruler's invasion, he was, to say the least, surprised. He gathered his forces and hurried northward. On September 25, the English entered the meadows of Stamford Bridge, their weapons "gleaming like ice" in the morning sun. As the two sides ordered their battle formations, King Harold is said to have sent an emissary to offer Earl Tostig a settlement if, for the sake of fraternity, he would change sides. When Tostig asked him what his brother would offer Harald Hard-Ruler, the emissary replied that the king had said something about seven feet of English soil. The offer was sharply declined.

The *Chronicle* then tells how, in the first place, the two sides were separated by a river, across which was a narrow bridge. A single Norwegian held the bridge, perhaps a berserk, and no infantryman or archer could dislodge him. Then an English soldier jumped into the river, and as he flowed downstream, he stabbed upward through the wooden planking, impaling the Norwegian. The English poured across the bridge to join battle.

The saga goes on to describe, somewhat improbably, how a mounted English force bore down on the Norwegians but seemed at first to make little impression.[16] Then the Norwegians countered and smashed through the English shield wall, and, again improbably, the English brought their cavalry into play while their archers fired salvos of arrows into the Norwegian ranks. Close-quarter fighting followed, and Harald Hard-Ruler hurled himself into the thick of the fray, slashing wildly with swords in both hands. As he did so, an arrow struck him in the throat, and he fell to the ground. Tostig set the Norwegian royal banner, "Landwaster," over him.

While Harald lay dying, the English king repeated his offer of peace to his brother, and again it was rejected. The battle resumed, and it soon became clear that the English were gaining the upper hand. The odds might have been leveled when a fresh host of Norwegians arrived from their ships, but they were so heavily armored that by the time they reached the English lines, many of them were too tired even to stand. Some died of exhaustion, and those who managed to shed their armor were hacked down. Leaderless and battered, the

Norwegians fled, with the English in pursuit. Night fell before the slaughter ended.

Later, when King Harold found the mangled body of his brother lying beneath his standard, he had his remains removed to York Minster for interment. The *Chronicle*'s account of the battle of Stamford Bridge concludes by telling how Harald Hard-Ruler's son, Olaf the Flashy, was given safe conduct to limp home with just twenty-four longships. As well as promises of future good conduct, he more than likely had to leave hostages behind him.

So it came about that Harold Godwinson won a great battle that he never imagined he would have to fight. Nineteen days later, the battle he had been preparing for all along took place three hundred miles away to the south, near a place called Hastings. Depleted after Stamford Bridge and drained by the rapid march south, Harold Godwinson's army, even with reinforcements, had little chance of defeating Duke William's fresh troops, and, without doubt in this instance, his employment of cavalry detachments. The Battle of Hastings on October 14, 1066, is rightly remembered as the most famous event in English history, for on this day Anglo-Saxon rule ended and French rule began. It is rather ironic that just a few weeks earlier, Anglo-Saxon England's 270 year Viking Age had also ended, but in such a way as to leave the country vulnerable to one last conqueror.

Conclusion

It has been argued that the centuries of Viking invasion had the positive effect of unifying England against a common enemy. But it could also be argued that the processes of national unity were already under way before the Vikings arrived: the greater kingdoms were absorbing the lesser ones, alliances through marriage were being forged, and there was already a unity of faith. The Vikings may have urged a common cause among free Englishmen, but they also baffled its progress with the division between north and south, and, for almost one hundred years, with the division between east and west.

There is also the matter of the scale of the devastation wrought by the Vikings. To the mayhem of rape and pillage, with which Vikings are commonly associated, one could also add the obliteration of two hundred years of Anglo-Saxon learning. During the late ninth century, when Alfred the Great set about reconstituting the monasteries, he acknowledged the Viking contribution to the difficulties he faced when he observed "how— before everything was ransacked and burned—the churches throughout England stood filled with treasures and books."[17]

Only through the ameliorating effect of Christianization did the Vikings begin to develop any respect for Anglo-Saxon civilization. From the late tenth century onward, Christian Vikings in England, the Scottish Isles, and Ireland were busily building and rebuilding churches and monasteries. The impact of the Viking Age in England, as elsewhere throughout the Viking world, was one that rebounded to good effect on the Vikings themselves.

One small example of this is provided by an inscription that surrounds a mid-eleventh-century stone sundial at St. Gregory's Minster in North Yorkshire. All the names of local provenance mentioned on it are of Scandinavian origin, and in a dialect that bears signs of the influence of Old Norse on the Anglo-Saxon tongue, it proudly asserts that

> Orm Gamalson bought St Gregory's Minster when it was all quite broken and fallen down and he let it be made new from the ground in honour of Christ and St Gregory in the days of King Edward and Earl Tostig.

Orm, a name meaning "serpent," rebuilt what his ancestors had either destroyed or caused to become derelict. Descendents of Vikings had become the benefactors of what their forbears once held in utter contempt.

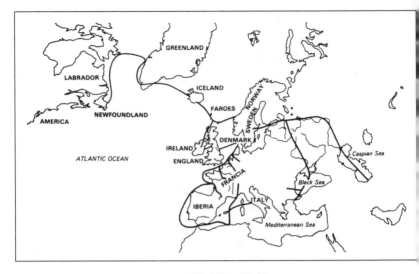

1 The Viking World.

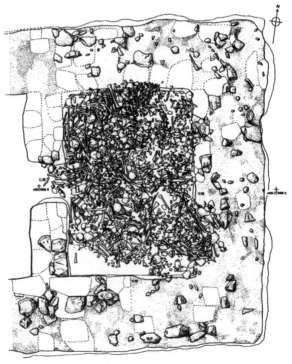

2 Drawing of the Repton burial chamber.

3 Scandinavia in the Viking Age.

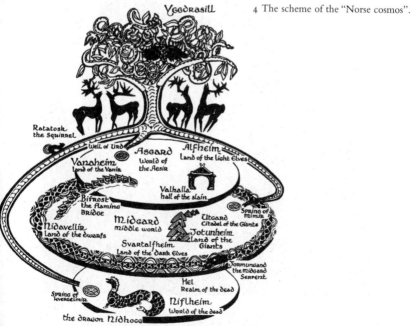

4 The scheme of the "Norse cosmos".

5 Viking Age double grave at Stengade, Langeland, Denmark. A bound and decapitated slave lies to the left of his master.

6 Realization by Gerry Embleton of the Viking sea battle at Hafrsfjord. Berserks wearing wolf skins are depicted in the foreground.

7 The late ninth-century Gokstad burial ship.

8 Early Raids on the British Isles.

9 Attacks on England 835–865.

10 England in 886.

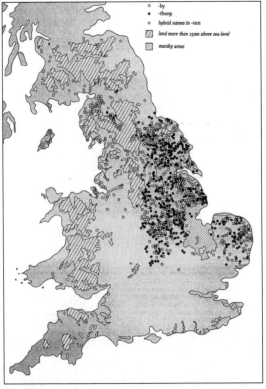

11 Distribution of
Scandinavian settlements
in Britain.

12 The Hon hoard, showing the Carolingian gold trefoil mount on the left.

13 Drawing of the Gosforth Cross in Cumbria. The face on the far right shows Odin being devoured by the wolf Fenrir. Beneath are images of the crucifixion of Christ.

14 The mid-eleventh century sundial at St. Gregory's Minster in North Yorkshire. The inscription tells how descendants of Vikings rebuilt the church during the reign of Edward the Confessor.

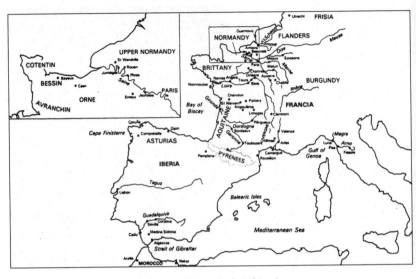

15 Western Europe in the Viking Age.

16 Viking Age Russia.

17 Tenth-century Icelandic parliament.

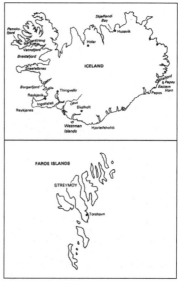

18 Viking Age Iceland and the Faroe Islands.

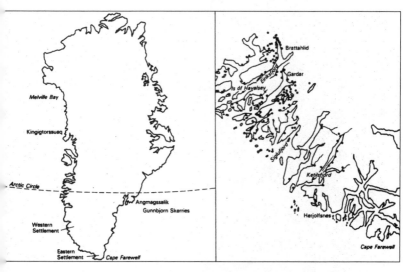

19 Greenland and the Eastern Settlement.

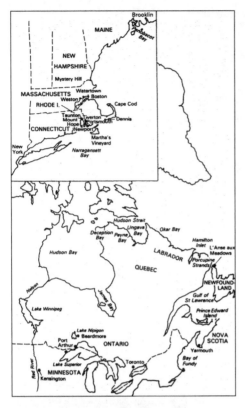

20 Vikings in North America

21 Statue of Leif Eiriksson in Reykjavik, Iceland.

CHAPTER 4

The Ravaging of Western Europe

On Christmas Day of the year 800, in St. Peter's Square, Rome, Pope Leo III crowned Charles of Francia as "Carulus Augustus," Charles the Emperor of the Romans. In effect, Charles was confirmed as the most powerful ruler in Europe since Julius Caesar. For over thirty years, Charlemagne (Charles the Great) had been building up his Carolingian Empire, which, in modern terms, encompassed Germany, Slovenia, Austria, Switzerland, much of Italy, the Netherlands, Belgium, parts of northern Spain, and, of course, France. Even the Orthodox Church of the Byzantine Empire acknowledged his singular authority in the West.

Charlemagne's main role, initially self-appointed but after 800 endorsed by the pope, was as defender of the Christian faith, in particular the Roman Catholic faith. His two chief enemies were his southern neighbors, the Muslim Arabs of Moorish Spain, and his northern neighbors, the pagan Germanic tribes of Saxony. Against the mighty and militarily sophisticated Arabs, he was obliged to settle for an uneasy border south of the Pyrenees, but against the Saxon tribes, he was less inhibited.

Having been subjugated by Charlemagne in 779, rebellious Saxons rose up three years later and annihilated the Frankish army on their soil. Charlemagne responded by taking into Saxony an army so large that the fearful populace promptly handed over 4,500 rebels at the town of Verden on the northern reaches of the River Weser. Charlemagne is said to have had them all executed. Only their leader, Widukind, escaped the butchery. Although in due course he would embrace the Christian faith and become Charlemagne's loyal vassal, Widukind's immediate response was to flee north and seek refuge among the Danes.

Exactly what Danish Vikings thought of their powerful Christian neighbors to the south is difficult to determine, but their opinions of Charlemagne can hardly have been improved by what they heard of his treatment of independently minded pagans. It was probably political misgivings rather than any kind of preparation for a retaliatory pagan-versus-Christian holy war that prompted King Godfred of the Danes to start fortifying his realm against possible intrusions from the Franks. Nevertheless, the divide between the Danes and the Franks was as ideological as it was political. And there can be little doubt that religious ideology played a major part in motivating Charlemagne to take similarly aggressive measures along his northern borders.

For fourteen years, up until Charlemagne's death in 814, Franco-Danish relations were, to say the least, strained. King Godfred massed his armies in a threatening manner in north Saxony and then began attacking any tribes in the Baltic regions that were collaborating with the Franks. Charlemagne responded by doing likewise to any tribes that openly showed favor to the Danes. Then, in 810, after several years of bellicose maneuvering, Godfred sent two hundred longships along the Frisian coastline, on the northwestern tip of the Carolingian

Empire, and not only took tribute from the residents but also boasted that he would now march on Aachen, Charlemagne's capital south of the Rhine. Only Godfred's sudden death stopped Charlemagne from invading Denmark. Instead, he sought and achieved a diplomatic solution with Godfred's son and heir, Hemming.

Diplomacy, in the sense of meddling with another's affairs to one's own advantage, remained Frankish policy when Louis the Pious inherited the empire in 814. Both military and economic backing was given to the Danish pretender Harald Klak, and this enabled him to take over the rule of much of Denmark. The fact that Harald was only a fair-weather friend was unforeseen, as was the consequence that dispossessed Danish aristocrats now looked to Francia in order to finance their domestic wars. The Viking fleet that "returned home with immense booty"[1] after raiding up the River Seine and down the coast of Aquitaine in 820 was more than likely captained by one such Dane who had fallen out of favor in his homeland.

While these sporadic Viking raids augured the shape of things to come, it was not Frankish foreign policy that caused their escalation; rather, it was self-induced Frankish vulnerability. The problem lay with the sons of Louis the Pious, and it was through their selfishness and bickering that the might of Charlemagne's once-great empire was squandered and plunged into civil war within twenty years of his death. The Vikings, as they often did, merely made the most of the situation that was presented to them.

Louis the Pious had three sons from his first marriage. The eldest, Lothar, was raised up as his co-emperor in 817, while the other two—Louis the German and Pippin I—were given subkingdoms. This arrangement in itself was not controversial. The difficulties really began when Louis the Pious was widowed and soon afterward married the Bavarian princess Judith. Their son, later to be known as Charles the Bald, was born in 823, and naturally Judith wanted the best for the child.

If Louis ever believed that making young Charles heir to the German territories would be acceptable to his other sons, he was quickly disillusioned. By 829, they had thrown him from power, and although he managed to reclaim his position two years later, the family crisis went from bad to worse. Large territories were allocated and reallocated, bitterness turned murderous, and the empire was going to rack and ruin. By the time Louis the Pious died in 840, Charles the Bald was as active as anyone in what had become a full-scale civil war. For there to be any hope of finding some form of stability, it became clear to all concerned that partitioning the empire into separate kingdoms was the only possible solution.

The brothers met at Verdun in 842, where a three-way split was agreed: Charles the Bald took the western territories in Francia proper; Lothar took the middle territories from Frisia down to northern Italy; and Louis the German took the east from Saxony down through Germany. The fourth son, Pippin, who had incurred his father's displeasure even more than the others, was effectively, and somewhat opportunistically, dispossessed. It would not prove to be a comfortable arrangement. Within a few short years, the old civil war merely became formalized as a threecornered war between kingdoms, with Pippin's son, Pippin II, making his own play for Aquitaine.

This, then, was the situation that the Vikings encountered in the 830s. Not only was there booty to be had from beleaguered Franks, already too embroiled with each other to defend themselves against marauders from the north, but the Viking invaders were also very often seen as weapons, which, once bought, the brothers could use against each other. For the Vikings, matters could scarcely have been better, and they came in huge numbers. The monk Ermentarius, a refugee from the despoiled monastery at Noirmoutier at the head of the River Loire, pinpointed the folly of it all.

> Their [the brothers'] strife gave encouragement to the foreigners. Justice was abandoned, and evil advanced. No guards were mounted on the beaches. Wars against foreign enemies ceased, and internal wars raged on. The number of ships grew larger, and the Northmen were beyond counting.[2]

The chief sponsor of Viking raiders from Denmark during the late 830s and the 840s was King Horik, who quickly perceived the opportunities that were opening up in Francia. Horik had seriously upset the Franks by protecting the deposed Harald Klak, who had allied himself first to Louis the Pious and then to Lothar and had then turned renegade and sacked the royal mint at Dorestad on the Rhine, as well as harrying across Frisia. Insult was added to injury when Horik offered to take over the running of Frisia from Louis the Pious. Given that Harald Klak, thanks to Lothar, was now monopolizing nearly all the trade moving down the rivers Rhine, Maas, and Schelde, this would have given the Vikings control over virtually all the Low Countries. It was an offer that Louis the Pious angrily rejected.

Horik's political insincerity and insolence turned to open hostility from 841 onward, when he sacked Rouen on the River Seine, and afterward the cross-channel emporium at Quentovic. As Horik appeared to get away with this without reprisal, he grew bolder as the decade progressed. According to the contemporary *Annals of St.-Bertin*, in 845 Horik sent six hundred longships down the Elbe with the intention of invading the East Frankish kingdom, but he was turned back by a Saxon army loyal to King Louis the German. Not wanting to go home empty-handed, Horik stopped off at Hamburg and attacked the great ecclesiastical center, forcing the religious community to flee with such valuables as they could carry. Among them was the revered missionary to the pagan north, Anskar.

After this, Horik returned to Denmark, but 120 of his longships, captained by a certain Ragnar, sailed into the River Seine and descended on Paris, seemingly indifferent to Charles the Bald's troops deployed on both banks of the river. When Ragnar took possession of one bank, he hanged over a hundred Frankish soldiers in full view of their horrified comrades on the opposite bank. So many deserted that Charles the Bald was forced to retreat to the Abbey of St.-Denis and pay over seven thousand pounds of gold and silver to prevent a massacre, but not before Vikings had ransacked the Abbey of St.-Germain.

Back in Denmark, Ragnar reported to Horik that the land was rich and fertile and the people cowardly. But Ragnar brought home more from St.-Germain than he had bargained for. Just as he was decrying Frankish courage, he suddenly fell to the ground, swelled up until he burst, and died. Plague was Ragnar's ultimate reward, and the *Annals* report that many other Vikings "were struck down by divine judgement with blindness or insanity, so severely that only very few escaped to tell the rest about the might of God."[3] Horik was deeply disturbed by what he regarded as the supernatural vengeance of the spirit of St. Germain, and he instructed that all valuables looted from Hamburg and Paris should be immediately returned.

While Horik was having second thoughts, freebooter Vikings in the Loire Valley were enjoying a heyday. Apart from the obvious benefits of pillage, many Vikings found lucrative employment as mercenaries hired out to noblemen who resented the rule of Charles the Bald. However, matters did not always go as these desperate noblemen intended. When Count Lambert set a party of Vikings against the town of Nantes, which he felt belonged to him, they exceeded their brief by killing everyone in sight—clergy and laity alike— and then carrying off everything of value to what had now become their permanent base at the abandoned monastery at Noirmoutier. The count's victory was thus achieved at the expense of those he had hoped to govern.

The ruination of Nantes represented in miniature what was happening right across the country. Amid the internecine strife, those who suffered most were the ordinary folk: "It was a crying shame," said the annalist, for while the populace was reduced to a diet of earth mixed with flour, "there was plenty of fodder for the horses of those brigands."[4] Taxed to penury by warring aristocrats and slaughtered without provocation by Vikings, the commoners were trapped between two evils. Those who formed their own militias and tried to deal with the Vikings on their own terms soon felt the backlash of their Frankish overlords. Great swathes of Francia became depopulated, and the tracks and byways were choked with refugees seeking food and shelter.

The Vikings were evidently so comfortably ensconced in the Loire Valley that they had time to contemplate what riches might be awaiting them to the south in Moorish Spain. Whatever information they had received about their chances in that direction was somewhat wide of the mark, as one party of about one hundred longships eventually discovered when it rounded Cape Finisterre in 844. Having been given a hostile reception in Christian Galicia, they pressed on down the coast of the Umayyad Emirate of Cordoba and attacked Lisbon. Then, in the approach to the Straits of Gibraltar, they laid waste to Cadiz and Medina Sidonia, and were sufficiently encouraged to sail inland up the River Guadalquivir and storm the Moorish capital of Seville.

So far, Viking successes against the Arabs had entirely depended on an element of surprise, but having taken Seville, they decided to settle for a while, in the belief that southern Spain could be exploited in exactly the same way as the Loire Valley. Surprise, they calculated, was no longer necessary. For the next five weeks, they set about looting the countryside, slaughtering any males they encountered and transporting the women and children to the island of Qubtil in readiness for the slave markets. While all this was going on, the Arabs had time to prepare a reply. Lookouts were posted, and a large army was assembled. This time, surprise would be on the side of the Arabs. The historian Ibn Kutia recorded what happened next, probably with a degree of exaggeration.

> At sunrise, the guard made known that a host of 16,000 *Madjus* was marching on Moron. The Moslems let them pass, cut them off from Seville, and cut them down. Then, our leaders advanced, entered Seville, and found its commander besieged in the castle.
>
> When the *Madjus* saw the Moslem army coming, and heard of the disaster that the detachment marching on Moron had met with, they

suddenly embarked. When they were sailing up the river towards a castle, they met their countrymen and when all these had also embarked, they all together began to sail down the river, while the inhabitants of the country poured on them curses and threw stones at them. When they had arrived a mile below Seville, the *Madjus* shouted to the people, 'Leave us in peace if you wish to buy prisoners of us.' People then ceased to throw stones at them, and they allowed everybody to ransom prisoners.[5]

Driven from Seville, the Vikings now took refuge on Qubtil, where they were besieged. Their only way of escaping with their lives was to free their hostages in return for food and clothing. Those Vikings who had been taken prisoner were hanged from palm trees in Seville. Others were beheaded, and it is said that two hundred Viking heads were sent as trophies to the emir's cousins in Tangier. The remnants of the Viking fleet that made it back to the Loire would have reported that Emir Abd-al-Rahman II was no Charles the Bald.

During the 850s, Vikings were ubiquitous in three areas of Francia: Frisia, the Seine basin, and the along the length and breadth of the Loire Valley. A temporary accord between the Frankish brothers led to a concerted effort to protect the northern territories from the likes of King Horik, who had apparently recovered from his superstitious misgivings. But in the central regions of West Francia, Vikings could only be combated in any conventional way when they gathered in large encampments. Here again, much depended on Charles the Bald being able to give the problem his full attention, and rarely was this the case.

In 858, Vikings returned to Paris and looted the Abbey of St.-Denis. On this occasion, they also carried off the abbot and his brother to their island encampment at Oissel, near Rouen.

Commanding the assault and kidnap was Bjorn Ironside, one of the feared Ragnarssons. Charles the Bald delivered 686 pounds of gold and 3,250 pounds of silver to Bjorn in order to ransom the captives. Infuriated and embarrassed, Charles had every intention of attacking Oissel and recovering his money. To this end, he had managed to co-opt his nephews into helping him. The whole project collapsed, however, when his half-brother, Louis the German, marched his army into West Francia looking for a confrontation. Thus, detained on other business, Charles decided to set a thief to catch a thief and hired a Viking leader called Weland to evict or, better still, kill Bjorn in return for five thousand pounds of silver.

Weland duly laid siege to Oissel and then, against Charles's express instructions, offered to let Bjorn go free. Weland's price for betraying his employer was six thousand pounds of silver, and Bjorn, rich from his Parisian adventure, happily paid up. The result was that Charles now had two wealthy Viking war bands dispersed around the Seine basin, neither of which could be trusted. Ermentarius again bemoaned the worsening situation:

> Everywhere there were massacres of Christians, raids, devastations, and burnings. Whatever the Northmen attacked, they captured without resistance: Bordeaux, Périgueux, Saintes, Limoges, Angoulême, and Toulouse; then Angers, Tours, and Orléans were destroyed.
>
> Then, a few years later, an almost immeasurable fleet sailed up the Seine River. The evil done in those regions was no less than that perpetrated elsewhere. The Northmen attacked the city of Rouen and devastated and burned it. They then captured Paris, Beauvais and Meaux, and they also levelled the castle of Melun. Chartres was also taken. They struck into the cities of Evreux and Bayeux and other neighbouring towns. Almost

no place, and no monastery, remained unscathed . . . and the kingdom of Christians succumbed.[6]

The frequent targets of these attacks were the monasteries, whose communities the Vikings held in utter contempt. This disdain is particularly apparent from the report of one raid on the Abbey of St.-Bertin, where the monks were tortured for mere entertainment, one being inflated with water and another used for spear practice.

After Oissel, Bjorn Ironside moved south into the Loire to link up with the one Viking whose reputation eclipsed even Bjorn's own: the Danish brigand Hastein. For the next thirty-five years, much of the havoc that the Vikings brought to bear on Western Europe can be traced to Hastein, and his impact on West Francia circulated in legend for centuries to come. In the early eleventh century, the French historian Dudo of St.-Quentin conjured the essence of Hastein's reputation in classical hyperbole.

> This was a man accursed: fierce, mightily cruel, and savage,
> Pestilent, hostile, sombre, truculent, given to outrage,
> Pestilent and untrustworthy, insolent, fickle and lawless.
> Death-dealing, uncouth, fertile in ruses, warmonger-general,
> Traitor, fomenter of evil, and double-dyed dissimulator,
> Conscienceless, proudly puffed up; seducer, deceiver, and hot-head.
> Gallows-meat, lewd and unbridled one, quarrel maintainer,
> Adder of evil to pestilent evil, increaser of bad faith,
> Fit to be censured not in black ink, but in charcoal graffiti.[7]

When Bjorn Ironside arrived from Paris, Hastein was already the terror of the Loire, but his thoughts had recently turned south toward Moorish Spain. It had been thirteen years since the calamitous Viking escapade in Seville, but Hastein was not the type to be dissuaded by the failure of others. With Bjorn Ironside partnering him, he began to assemble a great fleet.

In the spring of 859, Hastein and Bjorn set sail with sixty-two longships. Once again, Christian Galicians proved inhospitable, and further south, the Moors were standing by to prevent Hastein's fleet from getting far up the River Guadalquivir and so anywhere near Seville. Faced with intense opposition, Hastein and Bjorn moved south to Algeciras, where they burned down the great mosque, and then made the short crossing to Africa, where they rounded up dark-skinned natives who would bring a good price as "blue men" (*blámenn*) at the slave markets. Burning and looting as they went, they resumed their voyage around the Spanish peninsula and on to the coast of southern Francia. Here they settled for the winter on the island of Camargue, where, according to the Arab historian Ibn Adhari, "they took many prisoners, stole a lot of money and made themselves master of the city where they settled."[8]

The following spring, the Viking fleet entered the River Rhone and laid waste for one hundred miles as far north as Valence, until organized resistance forced a retreat. Then the fleet headed east along the coast toward Italy. Legend has it that Hastein's audacious plan was to attack the center of western Christendom at Rome.

Dudo of St.-Quentin gave a typically colorful, if rather formulaic, account of Hastein's activities in Italy. According to Dudo, as the fleet began to move southward along the coast of the Ligurian Sea, Hastein spotted the gleaming white walls of a fortified city. Believing this to be Rome, whereas it was in fact Luna some four hundred miles to the north, he set out a plan to take it. As there was no possibility of gaining the city by open assault, Hastein connived to gain entry Trojan-horse style. He would feign death and have Bjorn and his men pose as Christians seeking burial on sacred ground for their deceased leader. Moved by the strangers' plea, the compassionate townsfolk opened the great gates and admitted the "mourners" following the coffin. When the bishop and the duke of Luna stepped forward to officiate over the funeral, Hastein leapt from his coffin and slew them both. Only at this point did Hastein realize the shortcomings in his knowledge of Italy's geography. So embarrassed was he that he ordered the massacre of every one of Luna's male inhabitants.

It may well have been the case that after Luna and certain other devastating raids in northern Italy, Hastein's fleet sailed down past the boot of Italy and went on to vandalize towns and cities far away to the east on the Mediterranean fringes of the Byzantine Empire. What is more certain, however, is that their return journey to West Francia was the least lucrative part of their adventure. As the Viking fleet emerged through the Straits of Gibraltar, two things were waiting for them: a fleet of Moorish ships and, after that, extreme bad weather in the Bay of Biscay. The combination of these two adverse circumstances, and of further harassment by the Moors as they sailed north, resulted in a drastic reduction in the size of the Viking fleet.

Hastein and Bjorn returned to the Loire in 862 with approximately twenty longships. Compensating somewhat for the debacle off the coast of southwestern Spain was the easy money they picked up in Pamplona, Navarre, which they seized and ransomed back to the governor of the region for thirty thousand dinari. It had, nevertheless, been a voyage of very mixed fortunes, and this second bad experience at the hands of the Arabs meant that, hereafter, very few Vikings would try their luck in Moorish Spain, and none would ever again enter the Mediterranean from the West.

Bjorn Ironside parted company with Hastein soon after their return and is believed to have gone north into Frisia, although one source claims that he was with his brothers in the Great Army that invaded England in 865. Hastein remained to wreak havoc in the Loire Valley and to ally himself with rebellious Bretons, so bringing about the devastation of Poitiers, Angoulême, Orléans, and Le Mans.

But changes were afoot in Western Francia. Charles the Bald had finally realized that the Vikings could not be dealt with and had set about fortifying his realm with some urgency. Town walls were reinforced, rivers were defended with parapet bridges, and lieutenants were appointed to oversee the defense of the Seine basin and the Loire Valley, respectively. Only now did Charles ban the sale of weapons and horses to the Vikings.

These long-overdue defensive measures were not without effect, but they still did not prevent yet another Viking army from attacking Paris in 865. In this instance, it was probably just as much the payment of four thousand pounds of silver and an ocean of fine French wine that persuaded the Vikings to depart as it was the newly constructed river defenses. In either case, the upshot was that many Vikings now crossed the channel to ill-defended England, and for the next ten years, the Seine remained relatively free of trouble.

Not so, however, in the Loire. Hastein's alliance with the Bretons soon foundered, and when he turned on them and attacked Bourges and Orléans in 866, they were forced to buy peace for the price of five hundred head of cattle. The peace held for six years, during which time Hastein and his men showed a more neighborly mien. But old habits die hard, and Hastein was simply not cut out for life on the farm. So it was that in 872 Hastein managed to offend both the Bretons *and* Charles the Bald by taking the city of Angers.

Word that Hastein's army was on the way to loot and burn had caused the residents of Angers to evacuate, bleakly expecting to return once the damage was done and the Vikings were gone. Yet even these miserable hopes were confounded when Hastein simply sailed up the River Maine, through the open gates, and settled in as Angers's new owner. For a year, Hastein used Angers as a base from which he could mount raids on Brittany and then withdraw to safety. Charles, uniquely in alliance with the Bretons, laid siege but was unable to discomfit the Vikings. Then, in a move of uncharacteristic tactical brilliance, Charles set about diverting the great river. Left literally high and dry, Hastein was outsmarted, and, perhaps having negotiated certain incentives, he promised to quit the region for good. It was a false promise though, for he merely returned to his island lair at Noirmoutier. It would be ten more years before a huge army of Franks obliged Hastein to scurry from the Loire to the coastal regions in the north, and ten more years beyond that before he crossed the English Channel to take on the English—unsuccessfully, as things turned out.

When Charles the Bald died in 877, Charles the Fat, son of Louis the German, succeeded him. West Francia in the 870s had remained relatively free of Vikings—relative, that is, to the previous decade—and through the twists and turns of inheritance, the Carolingian Empire seemed to be reassembling. Yet when Vikings returned from England in significant numbers in 879 and began causing chaos in the northwest, Charles the Fat was evidently at a loss as to how to handle the situation. All the old tried, tested, and ultimately failed policies were revived. Vikings were bribed with cash and land and were hired to act as bulwarks against renewed Viking aggression coming from Frisia and Denmark. As a result, matters deteriorated in direct proportion to Charles the Fat's generosity.

The low point of his rule came in 885 when the greatest Viking fleet yet seen in Francia entered the Seine, captained by the Danish warlord known as Sigfred, who had already managed to extract 2,400 pounds of silver and gold from Charles in return for quitting his stronghold on the River Meuse. According to Abbo of Fleury's estimate—probably an overestimate—the fleet carried forty thousand Viking warriors. They smashed through the river defenses at Pont de L'Arche near Rouen and went on to surround the Paris stronghold of Île de la Cité, where a mere two hundred Franks were garrisoned under the leadership of Joscelin, the abbot of St.-Germain, and the redoubtable Count Odo.

The Vikings hurled every available force at the garrison. They attempted to destroy the stone and timber bridges that spanned north and south respectively, they used incendiary boats and siege engines, and they sought access by filling the moats with the dead bodies of men and beasts. Nothing availed. Then, in February 886, the swollen waters of the Seine brought down the weakened timber bridge, and many Vikings sailed through and went on to harry the region between the Seine and the Loire. But the siege still held. Finally, Count Odo managed to carry a message to Charles the Fat, who had been away in Italy, and in the early summer, Charles arrived and bought off the restive Sigfred, who was content with a mere sixty pounds of silver. Many Vikings considered the sum derisory and refused to budge.

Charles the Fat certainly had the opportunity to break the siege by force of arms, as was expected of him, but he had other, less dutiful, and certainly less heroic plans. Instead of confronting the Vikings, he made a deal with them: free passage to the southeast on the condition that they did as much damage as possible to the rebellious Burgundians. In addition, the Vikings would receive seven hundred pounds of silver on their return. Odo's and Joscelin's defense, which had cost Joscelin his life in the disease-ridden garrison, had been for nothing. Moreover, when the Vikings ignored Burgundy, preferring instead to ravage to the north, Charles still paid up as agreed.

Appalled Frankish nobles deposed Charles in 887, and he died under mysterious circumstances shortly afterward. The chances of reuniting the empire had now gone forever. Monarchies reasserted themselves, never again to be conjoined, and for a while West Francia was broken into two rival subkingdoms. Count Odo, hero of Paris, was set up to govern the area known as Neustria between the Loire and the Seine, while to the south, in Aquitaine, Charles the Simple, Charles the Bald's grandson, set himself up as Count Odo's rival. Yet, despite this fragmentation, both Odo and Charles the Simple were men of determination and mettle. The tide was turning against the Vikings.

During 888, Odo had several conspicuous successes, including overcoming Hastein at Montfaucon, but he was unable to prevent yet another attack on Paris a year later. In the end, a combination of force and, perhaps inevitably, bribery encouraged them to leave. More sophisticated fortifications and better-organized and more committed leadership were beginning to make a crucial difference; even so, no victory was decisive enough to bring about a complete Viking withdrawal. Then, in 892, nature took a hand when famine hit the country, and it was this, rather than any specific military campaign, that persuaded most of the Vikings to abandon Francia and head for England, Hastein included. There is some suggestion that the desperate Franks provided the ships.

Count Odo died in 898, and Charles the Simple was eventually able to reunite Neustria and Aquitaine under his kingship. For the next decade, something resembling calm descended. An indication that things might change for the worse came in 907, when the Breton leader Alan the Great died and the region was plunged into a power vacuum, destabilizing much of the territory to the north of Brittany. As was ever the case, Vikings back in Scandinavia saw the possibilities for personal advancement.

The Viking known as Rollo in French sources may have been Danish, or he may have been Norwegian. Icelandic sagas and histories that refer to Rollo as Hrolf the Walker, so named because he was too fat to mount a horse, suggest that he was the quintessential Viking warlord. Exiled from his homeland, at loggerheads with his father and brothers, and charismatically ruthless, Rollo's ambitions did not only involve amassing wealth but also conquering land. When Rollo crossed into the Seine basin in 911, he had no intention of leaving.

Rollo's first and only encounter with the army of Charles the Simple was at Chartres, approximately seventy-five miles southwest of Paris. Despite the fact that Charles was the victor, Rollo did not feel moved to abandon his schemes, and he simply went north and took over the battered trading center at Rouen on the Seine. Charles the Simple took the view that, rather than contest the matter, this new wave of Vikings could be used to defend Francia against any further interlopers from the north. Such thinking had in the past created more problems than it had solved, but Charles the Simple's plan was far subtler. He did not want merely to employ Rollo; he wanted to incorporate him. To this end, a peace treaty was agreed at St.-Claire-sur-Epte, and Rollo was named count of Rouen and given jurisdiction over several districts on the lower Seine. The Duchy of Normandy, the ducal lands of the Northmen, was thus founded.

As part of the treaty, or at least by 918, Rollo underwent an expedient baptism and was granted the hand in marriage of Charles's daughter, Giselle. In this way, Charles the Simple drew Rollo, the Viking pirate, into the illustrious line of Charlemagne and the world of the Frankish court with all its attendant pomp and circumstance. It was a brilliant political solution if not altogether an elegant one.

The late eleventh-century historian, William of Jumiéges, told how Rollo's investiture entailed one particularly deferential moment at which point Rollo was to kneel and kiss Charles the Simple's foot. This, of course, was not the Viking way, and Rollo would have none of it. Nevertheless, in the spirit of compromise, Rollo ordered one of his men to do it for him. When the moment came, Rollo's deputy dutifully stepped forward and, instead of kneeling, grabbed Charles's foot and raised it extravagantly to his mouth, thus catapulting the king backward, much to the delight of the common folk. As this story symbolically indicates, there was much work to be done before Rollo and his Vikings could move comfortably among the Frankish nobility. Yet Rollo was a fast learner, and records of his revitalization of Rouen as a trading and ecclesiastical center indicate something of his desire to be accommodated and, at least in terms of gestures, rehabilitated.

The impact of Rollo's presence was almost immediately felt among the Bretons, for when Rollo went to Rouen, certain members of his party went south into Brittany. Within a few years, Vikings had overrun the region with all the usual dismaying consequences, and when in 919 a Viking fleet arrived commanded by the Norwegian Rognvald, all remaining Breton aristocrats and clergy took flight for England. Soon afterward, Vikings were encroaching eastward as far as Burgundy. Rollo may have seen this as an excuse for him to break his solemn oath and start raiding north of Rouen. Although a confederacy of Frankish aristocrats quickly put a stop to his northward expansion, Rollo managed to exact important concessions in the form of further territories to the south. Normandy was spreading and would soon encompass Brittany. Freebooter Vikings in the region were simply absorbed.

Rollo died in or around 928, and despite the occasional resurgence of Scandinavian aggression, Francia's Viking Age came to an end. Among all the Vikings who eventually became part of European power structures, none can match Rollo's legacy. By the end of the century, Normandy was a secure powerhouse that spread from the borders of Picardy in the north to Brittany in the south. Less than a century beyond this, Normans in direct descent from Rollo were ruling over England and northern Italy. By then, there was little left of the loutishness that had caused Charles the Simple to be upended at Rollo's investiture. Normans became as French in manner and mode as the Franks had ever been.

Conclusion

Compared, for example, with Northumbria and East Anglia in England, the Viking imprint left on Francia was peculiarly light. There are a few traces of pagan Viking burials, the most notable being on Île de Groix off the southern coast of Brittany, where there was a ship burial of a Viking leader along with a sacrificed slave. At the center of the burial is a large iron cauldron. A few weapons, some gold and silver wire, a gold finger ring, and a few smith's tools surround it.

Other than this, archaeologists have recovered little more than a wide distribution of swords and spearheads, and from the repeatedly sacked trading center of Dorestad, a pair of gold arm rings. The most conspicuous signs of a Viking presence are found in the place-names of Normandy and Brittany, where, for example, Borneville signifies that the Viking Bjorn took over a rural estate, or where the element -*tot*, in Criquetot or Yvetot, signifies the Norse element -*toft*, meaning a homestead amongst agricultural land.

The reason there is such a dearth of material evidence is largely due to the way the Vikings used and abused the Frankish territories. Not until Rollo's establishment of Normandy did the Vikings make significant permanent settlement in Francia. For over one hundred years, Vikings exploited a situation of civil strife that had little or nothing to do with them. They were, in this respect, like parasites on an already diseased body. Much of what they plundered was taken home to Scandinavia and, given the shortage of Frankish valuables that have been found there, presumably melted down.

The notable exception is the Hon hoard that was deposited in Buskerud, Norway, during the mid-ninth century. Weighing five and a half pounds, the hoard mainly consists of gold Frankish coins that had been adapted as pendants, gold and silver beads, and interlace-style bracelets. Yet the most precious and exquisite of the objects in the hoard is an unusually large trefoil-shaped mount, regarded by experts as one of the finest surviving pieces of Carolingian gold work. Perhaps an object that once adorned a sacred shrine, it is a fitting symbol for how the descendants of Charlemagne reduced the glory of his empire to little more than scattered treasure for barbarians from the north to pick over and pocket.

CHAPTER 5

The Founding of Russia

According to the twelfth-century *Russian Primary Chronicle*, in 859, Swedish Vikings, known as both "Varangians" and "Rus," advanced down the rivers of Eastern Europe and laid many of the Slavic tribes under tribute.[1] A year later, the Slavs rebelled, and the Rus were driven back "beyond the sea." Discord ensued, and the Slavic tribes fell savagely upon each other. Unable to find peace among themselves, they decided to "seek a prince who may rule over us and judge us according to the Law." Whether it was the same Vikings that had previously been their oppressors or whether it was certain others is not clear, but it was to the Swedes, the Rus, that the Slavs sent emissaries saying, "Our land is great and rich, but there is no order in it. Come to rule and reign over us." In 862, three Rus brothers answered their call: "The oldest, Rurik, located himself in Novgorod; the second, Sineus, at Beloozero; and the third, Truvor, in Izborsk."[2]

This account encourages the belief that the founding of Russia, the settlement of the Swedish Vikings in Eastern Europe, was a charitable act performed to bring order to politically bewildered Slavs. While there can be little doubt that it was indeed Swedish Vikings who first established their presence at Novgorod, the manner by which they came to dominate the region may not have been so cordial, nor so late. Whoever Rurik and his brothers were—for we know nothing else about them—it seems unlikely that they would have waited for an invitation to exploit the phenomenal riches toward which the rivers of Eastern Europe could lead them. In all probability, what we have in the *Primary Chronicle*'s neat account is a foundation myth, a validation of twelfth-century dynastic entitlements. The *Primary Chronicle* is an invaluable document, but it is one that needs to be used with caution.

Aggressive Swedish movement east across the Baltic Sea can be traced in obscure legends dating from the seventh century, but it was as merchants and craftsmen during the eighth century that Swedes began permanent and peaceful settlement at bases such as Grobin and Elbing on the Baltic's southeastern shores. Items of jewelry of a distinctly Swedish character that have been recovered in and around these commercial ports suggest that Swedish families were comfortably situated among the local tribes.

During the mid-eighth century, the old Finnish trading post of Staraja Ladoga on the River Volkhov, eight miles south of Lake Ladoga, northeast of the Baltic Sea, was on the way to becoming the main transit point for Scandinavians trafficking between the Baltic and the Slavic territories. Staraja Ladoga soon attracted merchants from all points of the compass, carrying or seeking salt, amber, wax, honey, furs, and slaves. Ships could be refitted there, provisions could be loaded for long river journeys, and luxury goods were to be had in abundance.

It was at Staraja Ladoga that Swedish Vikings first saw the glitter of Arab silver and heard rumors from a thousand miles away of *Mikligard*, the "Great City" of Constantinople, the capital of Byzantium and jewel of the Greek Empire, whose population numbered in the region of one million. The urge to move south and meet with Arab traders face to face or see for themselves the gilded domes of Constantinople was irresistible. The rivers Dniester, Dvina, Lovat, Dnieper, and Volga that surge south and east through the Slavic regions were the highways that would, in due course, take them there.

Swedish Rus are known to have reached the southern shores of the Black Sea as early as 839, for the *Annals of St.-Bertin* record that the Byzantine emperor had arranged for a party of them to be safely escorted to Francia via the Mediterranean Sea. Somewhat flying in the face of received wisdom about the Vikings, these adventurers in the East were too fearful of the Slavs to make their way back to the Baltic alone and had thrown themselves on the mercy of the emperor. As other Rus travelers would find, getting to Constantinople was one thing, but having alerted the Slavs of their presence, returning directly northward was quite another. The next recorded visit by the Rus to Constantinople was some twenty years later. It was a far less agreeable occasion.

The founding of the Rus base at Novgorod may not have occurred quite as described in the *Primary Chronicle*, but it was perfectly within the logic of the trading potentials opened up by Staraja Ladoga. Novgorod is situated one hundred miles south down the River Volkhov, and a mere three miles north of Lake Ilmen, which gives access to the River Lovat and thereafter to the River Dnieper. By portaging their river-adapted longships between rivers and around rapids, the Rus could row to the Black Sea. Several sources confirm that on June 18, 860, a fleet of longships, estimated to have been two hundred strong, did precisely this.

Captaining the fleet were Askold and Dir, who had broken away from the Novgorod settlement and established themselves at the fortified hill town of Kiev, five hundred miles further down the River Dnieper.

Their arrival outside the walled city of Constantinople was fortunately timed, as Emperor Michael was detained elsewhere in his wars against the Arabs. When it became obvious to them that entry into the city was impossible, they set about doing what their contemporaries across Western Europe were doing. Outlying monasteries were plundered and burned, and men, women, and children were slaughtered without mercy.

Photius, the Byzantine patriarch, finally got word to the emperor, who hurried home. But despite managing to gain access to the city, Emperor Michael could do nothing to dismiss the Viking fleet. Contemptuously waving their swords aloft, Askold and Dir's warriors sailed past the city and headed down the Bosporus to the Sea of Marmora to desecrate the holy sites on the Islands of Princes.

Perhaps it was the Emperor's plans for a counterattack, perhaps the longships were full to overflowing with stolen goods and slaves, or perhaps, as the *Primary Chronicle* claims, it was the storm brought about by a nightlong vigil and the dipping of the Holy Virgin's vestments in the Black Sea that prompted Askold and Dir to leave. But whatever the reason they left, the shock and horror of this first taste of violence from the pagan north was not easily forgotten. Photius sermonized his dismay:

An obscure nation, a nation of no account, a nation ranked among slaves, unknown, but which has won a name from the expedition against us— once insignificant but now famous, once humble and destitute but now splendid and wealthy—a nation dwelling somewhere far from our country, barbarous, nomadic, armed with arrogance, unwatched, unchallenged, leaderless, has suddenly, in the twinkling of an eye, like a wave of the sea poured over our frontiers.[3]

There was clearly a suggestion that this was unlikely to be the last that Photius's flock would see of Byzantium's new neighbors in Eastern Europe.

News of Askold and Dir's wealth and prominence as rulers in Kiev soon reached Novgorod. Tensions were bound to have resulted, for two distinct Rus factions were now intent on controlling the same river passages used by traders moving north and south. Oleg, who succeeded Rurik in Novgorod in 879, took the view that there should only be one. He duly paid a visit to Kiev and invited Askold and Dir to meet with him. When they turned up prepared for diplomacy, he unceremoniously murdered them and installed himself in their place. From this point onward, Rus power became centered at Kiev.

Oleg appreciated that the key to success in the region was trade with the Greeks in Constantinople. Rus trade across the Black Sea doubtless increased during the latter part of the ninth century, but after the Askold and Dir affair, it was carefully monitored and conducted as trade between merchants, not between nations. It was this trade that Oleg wanted under royal Rus control. But there were difficulties. Oleg held sway over a region some seven hundred miles long, from Novgorod to the south of Kiev, and three hundred miles wide at its narrowest point. Much depended on keeping the Slavs in check, harvesting their trade goods, and taxing their wealth. Oleg appears to have achieved this within his kingdom, but the ferocious nomadic Pechenegs, who dominated the region north of the Black Sea, presented dangers for traffic between

Constantinople and Kiev. Moreover, the Greeks supported them as bulwarks against their enemies and as valued horse dealers. To gain the cooperation of the Pechenegs, Oleg again needed the cooperation of the Greeks.

It is very doubtful that Oleg used violence to persuade the Byzantine emperor to accept him as a trading partner in or around 907, as the *Primary Chronicle* boasts. If Oleg really did bully the Greeks into submission in typical Viking style, then it is surprising that no Greek historian ever thought it worthy of mention. What seems more likely is that when Oleg presented himself to the Greeks, perhaps with a display of force, the emperor had already seen the sense of a trade agreement. There were, however, certain judicious provisos. The Rus would not be allowed to take quarters inside the walled city, any violence from the Rus would find them subject to Byzantine law, and their movement in and out of the city would be strictly controlled: "They shall not enter the city save through one gate, unarmed and fifty at a time, escorted by an agent of the Emperor."[4] Memories of fifty years earlier still lingered.

Oleg died in 914. The Greco-Rus treaty of 907 had been ratified and elaborated in 912, and Oleg was said to have been "at peace with all nations." Consistent with this image of the benign elder statesman, the *Primary Chronicle* shrouds Oleg's death in the atmospherics of folktale. It is said that a court magician prophesied that Oleg's favorite horse would bring about his death, and as a precaution, Oleg sent the horse away. Years later, Oleg developed a sudden yearning to ride the horse again, but on hearing that it had since died, he commanded that its bones be reassembled so that for old times' sake he might once again straddle the beast. This he did, and on dismounting, he mocked the old prophecy by pushing over the skeleton and stamping on its skull. He did not notice until too late the venomous snake that slithered out of the splintered jawbones toward his foot.

Perhaps the *Primary Chronicle's* account of Oleg's demise is a parable that refers to Oleg's propensity for pushing his luck, for in reality his death was more than likely the result of an ill-fated assault on the Arabs, whose only experience of the Rus thus far had been as peaceful traders. While Oleg and the Byzantine emperor were firming up their trading alliance in 912, Oleg was simultaneously engaged in forming an alliance with the Khazars who controlled the wide territory between the Black and Caspian seas.

The religiously tolerant and divergent Khazars were the gatekeepers of all routes from the West into the Arab kingdoms. It was a lucrative position to hold, for no trader could pass through their lands without paying tax. It was, then, particularly foolish of them to jeopardize their position of trust and agree to give Oleg and his longships safe passage through their river ways in return for a half share of whatever he could plunder across the Caspian. As it later transpired, the Khazars were not only foolish but also deeply naive, for they had simply not expected the Rus to be so destructive.

Finding the Muslim lands south of the Caspian virtually undefended, the Rus ran amok. The towns of Abusgan and Ardebil were burned to the ground, outlying communities were ravaged, and thousands were massacred. When news of these atrocities reached the Khazar Muslims who dwelt around the northwestern Caspian, they assembled a great fleet and all but annihilated the Rus as they tried to reenter Khazar land. The unnamed Viking leader that Arab sources say perished in the reprisal was probably Oleg. This being the case, Oleg's favorite horse was greed.

Oleg's ward, Igor, succeeded him and was forced to spend the first five years of his rule suppressing Slav uprisings in the northwest of his realm and leading a campaign against the ever-troublesome Pechenegs in the south. Greek Byzantium was also enduring disruption, notably from attacks by the Bulgars in the 920s, and thereafter by the Magyars in the early 930s. The effect on trade was bound to have been damaging, and the old trading alliance appears to have become largely undone. In 941, Igor decided to rectify the situation by waging war on Byzantium.

Igor's first attack on Constantinople did not go according to plan. The *Primary Chronicle* tells how the Greeks had been forewarned of the Rus invasion by the Bulgars, and how an immense fleet of Greek galleys met the heroic Rus with "Greek fire" and forced them into retreat. However, the Byzantine diplomat Liudprand of Cremona, whose father had witnessed the event, reported differently. In Liudprand's version of events, the desperate and relatively defenseless emperor conceived of the idea of fitting out a few old galleys with flamethrowers, the so-called Greek fire, and leaving them apparently vulnerable to Igor's longships.

> As they [the galleys] lay surrounded by the enemy, the Greeks began to project their fire all around; and the Rus, seeing the flames, hurled themselves from their boats, preferring death by water to live incineration. Some sank to the bottom under the weight of their cuirasses and helmets . . . others caught fire even as they were swimming among the billows; not a man escaped that day, save those who made it to the shore.[5]

Rus survivors reported that the Greeks were in possession of "lightning from heaven" and were unconquerable.

Igor did not think so, and three years later he tried again, this time with Viking mercenaries from Sweden and the Pechenegs, among others from the Slavic tribes, augmenting his army. But the Greeks saw no point in a confrontation, despite being well positioned for one, and Igor got what he wanted—a resumption of the trade agreement that Oleg had enjoyed—without violence. Gifts of gold and silk were sent from the emperor, and Igor's army stood down.

The question now was what Igor would do with his coalition partners of Slavs and Swedish mercenaries. The Pechenegs and the other Slavic contingents were, in one sense, unproblematic, and, replete with Byzantine tribute, they either returned to their homelands or went west to relieve their pent up energies by harrying the Bulgars. But the Swedish mercenaries were a different matter. They had come in the belief that the spoils of a war against one of the wealthiest realms in the known world would, in time, be theirs for the taking, and they were not prepared to accept anything less. Igor suggested they go east.

While Igor prepared to send his envoys to Constantinople to conclude the new treaty, a large and covetous Viking army entered the Caspian Sea and sailed inland up the River Kura on its west coast toward the town of Berda. They overwhelmed or ignored the large but makeshift Arab army that harassed them from the rocky passes on either side of the river, and, having taken possession of Berda, they enslaved the women. With quite staggering condescension, they then offered to allow the Muslim townsfolk to continue in their religious practices, providing they accept Viking rule. The reply they received took the form of a shower of stones.

The Muslim women now set about plotting their revenge. Poison was insinuated into the Vikings' food and water supply, and soon the occupiers were laid low with dysentery. Many died, and in the squalor and the heat, the situation inside the town deteriorated day by day. Then, after repeated efforts to dislodge them, the Arab leader, Marzuban ibn Muhammed, managed to tempt those who remained onto open ground. Depleted and in poor shape, the Vikings were surrounded and butchered. Very few escaped to their longships.

The consequences of what the Vikings had done in Berda were soon felt in Kiev, for now the Khazars imposed a trade embargo, and the hostility of all Muslim people was guaranteed. Whatever trade advantages Igor had gained from his treaty with the Greeks, he lost the equivalent in the collapse of his trade with the Arabs. So, to make up his losses, Igor raised his taxes on the Slavs.

It was the Derevlian Slavs who balked at Igor's third demand for tribute from them within a matter of a few months and murdered him and his men on their last visit to Dereva in 945. It was a shock to the entire region, and the Derevlians surely knew that the Rus would not let matters lie. Desperately hoping to prevent what was surely inevitable, the Derevlians made an astonishing suggestion: Igor's widow, Olga, could be given the honor of marrying the Derevlian prince. There could have been no greater provocation, for the proposed political marriage would also have meant that the Derevlians would gain control of Igor's son and heir, Svyatoslav, and in this way the entire Rus kingdom. It was certainly the case, then, that the Rus were just as surprised as the Derevlians when Olga declared her willingness to accept a Derevlian delegation in Kiev to discuss the proposal. Not even her own people appreciated the depth of her cunning and her ruthlessness.

The first delegation duly arrived by boat, and Olga sent word saying that should they care to stay aboard, she would have them carried to the royal palace. The delegation approved the gesture, only to find themselves dropped into a trench in the great palace chamber and burned alive. Olga asked for a second delegation, and, oblivious of the fate of the previous delegation, they too rowed into Kiev full of expectations. This time, Olga asked if her noble visitors would like the use of the royal bathhouse before the start of the formalities, and once again the Derevlians took Olga at her word. As they filed into the bathhouse, the doors were sealed behind them, and the fires were set. Now Olga decided to take her vengeance into Dereva, where news of her murderous receptions had still not penetrated. At Igor's tomb, she had her bodyguard organize a great feast for the Derevlian aristocracy. The drink flowed, and the Derevlians warmed to their Rus hosts, little wondering why they appeared to remain sober. When the massacre began, no Derevlian was capable of stopping it.

Vengeance by stealth and deceit now turned to open warfare. The Rus cavalry forced the Derevlians back into their stronghold at Iskorosten, where Igor had been killed, and laid siege. The *Primary Chronicle* tells how Olga eventually offered to abandon the siege on payment of a tribute of three pigeons and three sparrows from each household, and how, when the birds were eagerly delivered, she had each of them fitted with a flaming match and then released back to their coops, so reducing the stronghold to ashes. Whether or not this common motif of legendary warfare in the ancient world was really one of Olga's ploys, it is unlikely that the

Derevlians were ever again in a position to complain about being overtaxed.

For the next twenty-four years until her death in 969, the remarkable Olga—an archetypal Viking queen—remained a powerful force in Rus affairs. She oversaw relations between Novgorod and Kiev, ensuring the pre-eminence of the latter, and founded numerous new trading posts. In 957, she visited Emperor Constantine Porphyrogenitus in Constantinople, who was alleged, rather improbably, to have sought her hand in marriage. Trade agreements with Byzantium flourished due to Olga's good offices, with the Greeks keen to purchase slaves, wax, and furs in return for gold, silks, and precious objects.

Yet the most significant feature of Olga's life for the future of the Rus was her conversion to Christianity. As the first royal Rus to take such a step, the precedent Olga set marked the beginning of the integration of the Rus, and thus the Slavs, into the broader politics of Christian Europe, but not quite yet. The Rus king, Olga's son Svyatoslav, was unconvinced by his mother's newfound beliefs and considered that such a faith would ill-befit a Rus leader in the Viking tradition. It was not integration that Svyatoslav hankered after but complete domination.

Svyatoslav's ambitious plan was to extend Rus territory west as far as the Danube and east as far as the Volga, so allowing him to monopolize all the trade routes running from the Baltic to the Black Sea and the Caspian. To do this, he had to take on the Khazars, the Bulgars—both western and eastern—and eventually Byzantium. At the outset, the political dynamics of the region favored him. The Greeks were distracted by their campaigns against the Arabs, and the Khazars, for so long the defenders of the Muslim east against any further Rus aggression, were experiencing disunity within their realm, so much so that certain factions approached Svyatoslav for his assistance. There was just one dynamic that did not favor Svyatoslav, and that was the implacability of the Pechenegs. Leaving this out of the equation proved to be his Achilles' heel.

In 964, "stepping lightly as a leopard,"[6] Svyatoslav sailed due east from Novgorod along the River Volga into the heart of East Bulgar territory, which he rapidly overran. Then he sailed south to the Khazar capital of Itil, where the Volga enters the Caspian. The assault on Itil was in many ways the last straw for the Khazars, and they never again recovered their power in the region. The first stage of Svyatoslav's campaign had been completed with relative ease.

Svyatoslav now looked to the West Bulgars, who controlled trade down the River Danube. For this next stage of his campaign, he received material encouragement from the Greek emperor, who was delighted that the Rus should tackle his West Bulgar enemies while he was detained in his wars against the Arabs. What he did not fully appreciate was Svyatoslav's intention of establishing a new Rus capital at the town of Pereyaslavets on the Danube, where he judged that all riches were concentrated.

Had the emperor realized that this would be the outcome, his support may well have been for the devil he already knew. The Rus conquest of the lower Danube territories was as rapid and complete as their conquest of the territories in the East. Within three years, Svyatoslav had trebled the size of Rus dominions and was now, he believed, in such a position of strength that even Byzantium lay within his grasp. Then the Pechenegs took a hand.

With Svyatoslav and the Rus army absent, the Pechenegs saw their chance and swarmed north and surrounded the walls of Kiev. Olga and her grandsons were trapped inside. Svyatoslav had no alternative but to quit his new capital and hurry back to break the siege. The Pechenegs were quickly dispersed into the steppes, and Svyatoslav immediately began to prepare for his return to Pereyaslavets. His neglected subjects did not approve, and the aging Olga sharply reminded her son where his duty lay—beside her in Kiev.

She had a point, for Novgorod was on the brink of declaring itself independent, as were other major centers across the Rus kingdom, and even Kiev was becoming unstable. Svyatoslav's suggested remedy was to appoint his three sons to act as his regents in his absence, allocating to each of them principalities in Kiev, Novgorod, and Dereva. But Olga, perhaps sensing that in due course her grandsons' new roles would lead to bitter rivalry, would have none of it. Only when she died two years later did Svyatoslav feel free to put his plan into effect and return to Pereyaslavets. In the meantime, however, things had changed.

When Svyatoslav returned to the Danube, he found that the Greeks had taken measures to prevent him from picking up where he had left off. Marriage alliances had been made between the imperial Greek and royal Bulgar families. In the yearlong campaign that followed, Svyatoslav showed that he could be both ruthless and politically skillful. He persecuted those Bulgars who had allied themselves to the Greeks, impaling, so it is said, twenty thousand of them, but when he captured the Bulgar royal family in Preslav, he saw the diplomatic sense of offering them his protection. Then he took his army deep into the mountainous regions to the west of Constantinople and ransacked and burned the towns of Adrianopolis and Philippopolis. A direct confrontation with the Greeks was now inevitable.

In the summer of 971, the great armies of Emperor John Tzimisces and Svyatoslav finally faced each other across the dusty level plains outside the town of Dristra (modern Silistra) on the Danube, where the Rus had established their headquarters. Fighting alongside the Rus was a vast throng of Slavic mercenaries, including, rather bizarrely given recent history, a contingent of Pechenegs. Few stayed longer than the first battle, which went the way of the Greeks, albeit not decisively. Weeks of skirmishing and pitched battles followed, with the Rus unable to break out of Dristra but always able to retreat within the walls when matters got awkward. It was not a good situation, and Svyatoslav knew that either he had to escape or suffer the attrition of an unbreakable siege.

On July 24, 971, Svyatoslav launched a furious attack, forcing the Greeks to pull back. But luck was against the Rus. A great storm blew up, bringing confusion and chaos to the battlefield. The Greeks regrouped and counterattacked as the storm subsided. Legend tells how the Greeks were inspired by a mysterious rider on a white charger, who they later believed was sent to deliver them by the Holy Virgin. Svyatoslav, wounded and weary, retreated to Dristra, where, according to Greek sources, he raged all night in anger and pain. The following morning, he offered terms that Emperor John willingly accepted.

The Rus and Greek leaders met on the banks of the Danube to agree to a treaty. A Byzantine official, Leo the Deacon, was present and later described the arrival of the Rus leader.

Svyatoslav crossed the river in a kind of Scythian boat; he handled the oar in the same way as his men. His appearance was as follows: he was of medium height—neither too tall, nor too short. He had bushy brows, blue eyes, and was snub-nosed; he shaved his beard but wore a long and bushy moustache. His head was shaven except for a lock of hair on one side as a sign of the nobility of his clan. His neck was thick, his shoulders broad and his whole stature pretty fine. He seemed gloomy and savage. On one of his ears hung a golden earring adorned with two pearls and a ruby set between them. His white garments were not distinguishable from those of his men except for cleanness.[7]

By contrast, Emperor John arrived wearing golden armor, not that this impressed Svyatoslav: he may have been offering terms, but he was not acknowledging defeat and was certainly not acknowledging any betters. The pagan chieftain and the Christian emperor sat together on the main thwart of the Rus longboat and agreed to maintain "peace and perfect love." What this meant in the short term was that Svyatoslav would depart with the booty he had won on the Danube, and in return the Greeks would encourage the Pechenegs to allow the Rus safe passage back to Kiev.

Svyatoslav and his men reached the lower Dnieper as the winter of 971 began to bite. Food ran short, and local Slavs were able to charge as much as half a pound of silver for a horse's head. News spread of the weary Rus heading north, laden with treasure. Maybe Emperor John's request to the Pechenegs to allow the Rus safe passage never got through, maybe it was ignored, or maybe it was never made, but in the spring of 972, the Pechenegs discovered the Rus trying to negotiate their boats around a set of rapids and fell on them. As was their way when honoring a great fallen enemy, they made a drinking vessel of Svyatoslav's skull.

The death of Svyatoslav was in many ways the end of an era. There would be no more expansion southwest toward the Danube, and apart from a serious, although only temporary, lapse in good relations between Kiev and Constantinople in the mid-eleventh century, the Rus and the Greeks became largely reconciled. Cementing the accord were marriage ties and, most significantly, the wholesale adoption of Orthodox Christianity across the Rus domain. Slow processes of assimilation brought about some of this. As the names of the Rus rulers suggest, Scandinavian identity—culturally and linguistically—had gradually given way to a Slavic identity, and thereafter to a Slavic identity within a Christianized context. There were also pressing economic reasons to seek greater security by fostering good relations with Byzantium. A main source of Rus wealth, and indeed Viking wealth generally, suddenly dried up in the late 970s when Arab silver mines ceased to be productive. The processes of cultural osmosis were certainly hastened by the need for a reliable income.

Much of this integration came about during the reign of Vladimir, who finally came to power after six years of bloody competition with his half brothers for the right to succeed Svyatoslav. He was an unpromising candidate for Christian conversion, a heavy drinker, a human sacrificer who idolized the Slav gods, and a notorious and insatiable womanizer. But in 988, the promise of the emperor's daughter, Anna, along with her Crimean territories by way of a dowry, were sufficient to convince Vladimir of the merits of Christianity, and he ensured that his own conversion was followed by that of all his subjects. Nevertheless, marriage into the empire presented one minor problem in the form of Vladimir's long-suffering Swedish wife, Ragnheid. One account says he bought her off by building the town of Izaslavl for her and their son; another says he packed her off to a convent. Either way, Ragnheid's life probably improved.

The old Rus urge to expand was satisfied to some degree by Vladimir's attacks on the East Bulgars during the early years of his rule, against which the Greeks set no obstacles. Perhaps he hoped to find some economic compensation for the shortage of Arab silver, in which case he would have been disappointed. But, this apart, Vladimir was far too preoccupied with dealing with insurgencies in his own realm, and, as ever, with trying to keep the Pechenegs at bay, to pursue expansionist goals. Consolidation and political acceptance were the achievements of Vladimir's rule.

In 1015, Vladimir died, and turmoil once again broke out over the succession, this time pitting the appointed heir, Jaroslav, against his usurper brother, Svyatopolk. Jaroslav eventually gained the upper hand in 1019, and with it the title of Grand Prince of Russia. Following on from his father's example, Jaroslav—later known as Jaroslav the Wise—expanded his political alliances. He married Ingigerd, the daughter of the Swedish king Olof Skötkonung, and their daughter, Ellisif, went on to marry Harald Hard-Ruler, the future king of Norway. Harald's half brother, the posthumously sainted Olaf Haraldsson, sought refuge with Jaroslav in the year immediately preceding his ill-fated attempt to reclaim the Norwegian throne in 1030, and Magnus, Olaf's son, remained in Jaroslav's safekeeping until he could return north to rule over the lands his father had lost. As had long been the case economically, Russia was now meshed to both the north and east of Europe politically.

Besides this, Jaroslav was determined to establish the particular cultural character of his kingdom. Rather than model

Russia along Byzantine lines, he saw to it that religious texts were translated into the Slavonic language, and he reinforced Vladimir's ruling that a Slavonic, and not a Greek, liturgy should be heard by the Russian faithful. Monasteries and churches proliferated, the crowning architectural glory being the great cathedral of St. Sophia in Kiev, guarded by the impregnable Golden Gate fortification. Jaroslav's reign was very much that of the enlightened and progressive European ruler. Only one event marred his otherwise politically astute rule.

The reason why Jaroslav the Wise took the uncharacteristically unwise decision to send his son into the Black Sea in 1043 to take on his longtime allies the Greeks has three interrelated explanations. First, since the time of Vladimir, elite Viking mercenaries known as the Varangians had been sent in their thousands to the aid of the Greek emperors. They were, however, high maintenance, and the current emperor, Michael, may well have thought that Rus brokerage in this regard more advantaged them than it did him. His refusal to use them was an affront and an embarrassment to Jaroslav. Second, much to Jaroslav's annoyance, a breakaway Rus faction was being harbored in Constantinople. Third, Emperor Michael was perceived as being weak. Viking opportunism was not far from the surface of the noble countenance presented by the Grand Prince.

Whether punitive or exploitative, this last Rus attack on the Greeks was at least as disastrous as the worst of any previous attacks. A violent wind blew the Rus longships hither and thither, and the more stable Greek galleys were able to pick them off using their lethal incendiaries. According to the Greek historian Cedrenus, fifteen thousand Rus corpses littered the Bosporus. It took three years before amity was once again restored.

Jaroslav's reign marked the acme of the early Russian kingdom. Lithuanians and Poles soon learned that Russia was not a country that tolerated offense or lack of cooperation, and any Slav tribe that dared express hostility or failed to deliver tribute was brutally suppressed. By the time Jaroslav died in 1054, the political alliances that he had formed across Europe, the belligerence he had shown toward weak or unhelpful neighbors, and the strict control he had exercised over domestic affairs ensured that Russia became an established geographical fact in Europe that none could deny.

Conclusion

Some indication of the scale of the commercial transactions that were stimulated by the Rus is offered by the coin hoards found in the Swedish homeland. Over half the Arab silver in the form of dirhem coins, and over three-quarters of the Byzantine coins that have been discovered in Scandinavia, were deposited for safekeeping in Gotland, the Swedish-owned island in the Baltic. Here, thirty-two coin hoards have been unearthed dating from before 890, and from the tenth century, a further ninety thousand coins, most of which originated at the mints in Tashkent, Samarkand, and Baghdad. This, however, does not mean that the gold and silver bonanza that resulted from trade in the East was only beneficial to the Swedes, as most coinage would, in the course of its movement west, have been melted down into ingots or reworked for ornamental purposes.

In reality, the commercial activities of the Rus would have meant transactions involving millions of silver and gold coins, as well as a vast store of Russian fixed-weight silver neck and arm rings known as *grivna*. Portable, immediately exchangeable, and rare, precious metal from the East galvanized the economies of all three Scandinavian countries and can be credited as having financed the Viking expansion for well over a hundred years.

For some—the strong, the lucky, and the wellborn—the riches of the East were literal. Yet for the majority of those who were either raised in the Rus kingdoms or lured there by the prospect of great wealth, life in the frontier towns of early medieval Russia was tough and dangerous. In the early tenth century, the Arab writer and traveler Ibn Rustah reported on a visit he made to Novgorod.

Russia is an island around which is a lake, and the island in which they dwell is a three days' journey through forests and swamps covered with trees and it is a damp morass such that when a man puts his foot on the ground it quakes owing to the moisture.

They have a king who is called Khaquan Rus, and they make raids against the Saqalaba [Slavs], sailing in ships in order to go out to them, and they take them prisoner and carry them off to Khazar and Bulkar and trade with them there.

They have no cultivated lands; they eat only what they carry off from the land of the Saqalaba.

When a child is born to any man among them, he takes a drawn sword to the new-born child and places it between his hands and says to him: 'I shall bequeath to you no wealth and you will have naught except what you gain for yourself by this sword of yours.'

They have no landed property nor villages ... their only occupation is trading in sables and grey squirrel and other furs ... and they take as the price gold and silver and secure it in their belts or saddle bags.[8]

We hear, too, of Rus traders too fearful of robbers of their own race to venture into public without bodyguards. All this, of course, is some distance from the images of the opulence and grandeur of the Rus courts that are presented in the *Primary Chronicle*.

The romance of the East remained strong in the Scandinavian imagination for centuries to come, and Icelandic saga writers of the thirteenth and fourteenth centuries told tales of east-bound Vikings encountering trolls, giants, dragons, beguiling witches, and treasures beyond dreams. Not all were fantasies, and certain tales of exotic Russia had a basis in historical truth, such as the *Saga of Eymund*, which dramatizes the problems that unattached Varangians could have on Rus internal politics, and the *Saga of Yngvar the Widefarer*, whose eponymous hero met his true love and his death in Serkland, the land of the Saracens east of the Caspian Sea, in 1041.

But the real history of the Vikings in the East was no less sensational. One figure in particular seems larger even than legend. As was recorded in Snorri Sturluson's history of the Norwegian kings, *Heimskringla*, it was from Jaroslav's Kiev that Harald Hard-Ruler went on to achieve the highest possible rank in the Greek emperor's Varangian Guard, and so to gather the greatest fortune ever seen in the Old North. It was this exceptional wealth that not only secured him the Norwegian throne in 1046, but also caused him to believe that he had the wherewithal to conquer England in 1066. It is fitting that Harald, son-in-law to Jaroslav the Wise and truly the last of the Vikings, should have launched his career in a realm that was entirely manufactured by Viking adventurers.

CHAPTER 6

Settlements Across the Atlantic: Iceland, Greenland, & North America

In *The Saga of the Greenlanders*, it is said that in or around the year 1000, a single longship sailed west from the southern tip of Greenland. Captaining the crew of thirty-five was Leif Eiriksson, son of Eirik the Red, the founder of the Greenland colony and an exile from both Norway and Iceland on account of his murderous temper. Whilst Eirik the Red's violent and adventurous career would be celebrated as being quintessentially Viking in Icelandic sagas of the thirteenth century, immortality would ultimately belong to his son, for the westward voyage of Leif Eiriksson led him to become the first European known to have to set foot on the North American continent.

Whether Leif 's journey was a deliberate voyage of discovery or whether, as is said in *Eirik the Red's Saga*, it was the result of violent winds that drove him hundreds of miles off course during a journey from Norway to his home in Greenland, Leif's discovery of the eastern seaboard of a vast new continent was, in effect, the culmination of almost two hundred years of westward expansion by Viking seafarers. What evidently motivated Norwegians to take their chances on unknown and uncharted seas were a thirst for independence and the need for new land. When Leif Eiriksson looked inland up a river teeming with salmon, and when his men discovered vines growing wild, Leif must have thought he had reached the land of plenty. Although his expectations of what could be achieved in the place he called Vinland were soon frustrated, the story of how Viking adventurers came to discover North America is one of truly epic proportions.

It begins in the general expansion of the Viking Age as it developed during the ninth century. Little if anything beyond vague rumors and legends were known of the Atlantic islands before the Vikings moved aggressively south and west toward Britain and Ireland. Yet, once discovered, the opportunities these remote windswept places presented for unopposed settlement immediately attracted them.

Roughly equidistant from the Norwegian fjords and Scotland are the Shetland Isles, which Vikings had used as staging posts for their assaults around Britain's coastline since the late eighth century. Approximately two hundred miles northwest of Shetland are the Faroe Isles, an archipelago of around twenty islands, the largest, Streymoy, covering some two hundred square miles. Scandinavians were not, however, the first adventurers to appreciate the lush pastures and teeming wildlife of the Faroes, and Irish monks seeking the meditative life had settled there since the early eighth century. But these peregrine Christian hermits presented no obstacle to the rugged land takers who rode before the Atlantic storms and disembarked there in the first quarter of the ninth century. The Irish monk Dicuil lamented what was reported to him:

There is another set of islands, nearly all separated by narrow stretches of water; in these for nearly a hundred years hermits sailing from our country, Ireland, have lived. But now just as they were always deserted from the beginning of the world, so now because of the Northmen pirates they are emptied of anchorites, and filled with countless sheep and very many diverse kinds of sea-birds.[1]

The colonization of the Faroes was in one sense a matter of fortunate accident, more a consequence of the wild winds that blew Viking longships off course than a planned migration. If legend is to be believed, the same was also true of the settlement of Iceland early in the second half of the ninth century. However, in this case, explicit political grievances brought about by Harald Finehair's determination to unite Norway under his kingship provided a more urgent context. What resulted was the most remarkable colony in Scandinavia's medieval history.

The Icelandic land registry, the *Book of the Settlements*, tells of three mid-ninth century seafarers who came across a large, seemingly uninhabited island six hundred miles west of Norway. It was the last of these, a certain Raven Floki, who, with his men, spent his summer harvesting an abundance of salmon from Iceland's large rivers but barely managed to survive the winter there. Disgruntled by the hardships he endured, it was Raven Floki who gave the country the unflattering name by which it is still known. Yet not all of his company was so critical, and one of them reported that "butter dripped from every blade of grass."[2] While this latter report may have excited the interest of some back in Norway, it was not until the late 860s that the foster brothers, Ingolf and Hjorleif, fugitives from Norway, resolved to make Iceland their home. It turned out to be a violent start to a colony that, in years to come, would give the subject of violence the highest possible literary expression.

Ingolf opted to make his first camp among the craggy inlets of Iceland's east coast, whereas Hjorleif rounded the southeastern tip of the country and sailed west in the hope of finding more congenial terrain. Accompanying him were a number of Norwegian shipmates and their wives and a dozen Irish slaves. When Hjorleif decided to put ashore and establish a settlement, he set the slaves to work plowing the rubble-strewn land, much to their disgust. Their rebellion and flight included the murder of Hjorleif and his companions and the abduction of their womenfolk. Ingolf soon got word of his foster brother's death, and he and his men set out in pursuit of the culprits, finally coming upon them on an island not far from Hjorleif 's deserted settlement. In the time-honored manner of the blood debt, Ingolf took his revenge. Then, still resolved to make Iceland his home, he sailed along the breadth of the south coast and turned north. As a devout pagan, Ingolf cast his temple pillars overboard with the intention of letting the gods guide him to good land. He recovered them in a natural harbor backed by low-lying fields and, in the distance, a reeking volcano. This would be Ingolf 's stead. He named it Reykjavik, "Smokey Bay."

Meanwhile, back in Norway, civil war was brewing. Harald Finehair's monarchic ambitions looked to many like tyranny, especially to the men of the western fjords, who deeply resented Harald's usurpation of their inheritance rights. This would culminate in a sea battle between the aspiring king and resentful chieftains at Hafrsfjord in or around 885. Harald, however, would triumph, and this doubtless spurred many to follow in Ingolf's wake. But many others had long ago seen the way matters were tending, and the settlement of Iceland was already under way a decade before Harald's ascendancy at Hafrsfjord. Whether or not the migrants were antimonarchists or simply eager to carve out a new future for themselves, as the century drew to a close, what had begun as a steady flow had become a flood.

By 930, the population of Iceland numbered twenty to thirty thousand, and little in the way of good land was left to be taken. With newcomers still pouring into the country, tensions between neighbors, between early and late settlers, and between powerful families and poor farmers were becoming critical. Law and order needed to be established. Remarkably, the settlers founded a republic.

The Icelandic Republic, or Commonwealth, as it is more widely known, was based on a judicial system that was inaugurated at the grand annual parliament, or Althing, about thirty miles north of Reykjavik. In due course, further assemblies, or Things, were established in the regions. These met more frequently and could refer unresolved cases to the Althing. Every free man, no matter what his economic standing, could have representation at a Thing; though, for justice to be done, powerful patronage from the priest-chieftains was invariably necessary. Although those who commanded force of arms in order to protect vested interests could often distort or disdain legal proceedings, the democratic principles that, almost a thousand years later, came to underlie the governance of the United States of America and many European nations were first enshrined in tenth-century Iceland.

The decline of the Icelandic Commonwealth was slow but inexorable. European kings and the increasingly powerful

offices of the church soon came to regard Iceland's persist-
ent paganism and anomalous republicanism as uncomfortable,
perhaps even as a dangerous precedent. By the year 1000, the
pressures to conform, at least in terms of religious practice,
were overwhelming. At stake was the whole economic future
of the island, for Norway's king had it in his power to ruin
the settlers through trade embargoes. The Althing met, and
for three days the Lawspeaker, chief among the legislators,
considered how Christianity might be introduced in the face
of considerable opposition among many of the settlers. In
the end, concessions were made to practicing pagans, and
the country adopted the new faith as its official religion. As
a consequence, the role of the chieftains was redefined. They
were no longer pagan priests but guardians of the church, its
authority, and, significantly, its revenues. For men of ambition,
the opportunities for self-advancement and corrupt dealings
were huge.

It took another 250 years before the fabric of Icelandic
self-governance unraveled into civil war, by which time the
ambitions of Norwegians kings to annex the island were not
only naked but, in the end, also welcome. In 1262, or shortly
thereafter, the Icelandic Commonwealth ceased to be, and
Icelanders became subject in all meaningful senses to Norway.
It had been an extraordinary period in early European history,
and one that, as the Icelanders clearly recognized throughout,
merited a detailed history. The legacy they bequeathed to
posterity was just that, and the unique form it took is the vast
body of literature known as the Icelandic sagas.

The adoption of Christianity brought Icelanders into direct
contact with the transmission processes of the Christian world.
In short, this meant the Roman alphabet and the power of

the written word. Icelanders readily absorbed the subtleties of European scholarship and the infinite expressive possibilities of a chirographic culture. By the beginning of the twelfth century, Icelandic intellectuals had written a grammar of the Old Norse tongue, and monastic schools were building up libraries and writing Latin hagiographies of Icelandic bishops. As time went on, Old Norse became the medium of expression, and the subject matter widened to include accounts of the lives of Norwegian kings, often emphasizing the role of Icelandic warriors and poets in monarchic affairs. Oral traditions were frequently the chief source for these histories, and among the material that was transferred to the page were the sacred traditions, beliefs, and legends of the pagan past. A literary culture—vibrant and learned—was well established by the early thirteenth century.

Whether it was the need to demonstrate historical continuity, or whether it was a deep-seated national anxiety about the increasing chaos that the commonwealth was experiencing, the predilection among Icelandic writers for reflecting on the past soon found its focus on the lives of the early settlers. Whatever motivated their production, the so-named Icelandic Family Sagas were the acme of medieval Icelandic authorship. Set, for the main part, in the period that spanned the establishment of the law in 930 and the decades following the conversion to Christianity in 1000, the Family Sagas gave expression to the central problems of the age. On the one hand, they show admiration for heroic individualism, and on the other, they articulate the crucial importance of community fellowship and the law. As the pacifist Njal declared in the saga that bears his name, "With law shall our land be built up, with lawlessness laid waste."[3] Unhappily, this sentiment did not prevent Njal and his family from being burned alive in their homestead.

In these finely crafted and complex works of historical reconstruction, more resembling the modern novel than the cycles of high romance that were current throughout the rest of medieval Europe, issues of personal honor and community responsibility come into violent conflict. The result is invariably tragic, and succeeding generations often find themselves carrying forward the grievances of the previous one, sometimes willingly, sometimes not. Conflicts break out over land entitlements, inheritance rights, sexual jealousy, religious superstition, and heroic posturing, in which the central characters are forced to confront moral contradictions of their own making. The Icelandic Family Sagas are, in a sense, a meditation on loss, or perhaps, more specifically, on the glory and the poignancy of one of the great moments in the history of early medieval society. Dryly ironic and psychologically convincing, they are quite rightly judged to be in the top rank of world literature.

It is not difficult to appreciate why Icelandic authors chose the tenth and early eleventh centuries in which to set their Family Sagas, for it was then that the land seemed full of promise. Yet, as the sagas typically observe, promise is frequently disappointed, and hopes are often dashed. Such was the case for many of the economic migrants and outcasts that came to Iceland late in the tenth century. Among them was Eirik the Red.

The two Icelandic sagas that tell of Eirik's life and that of his descendants—*The Saga of the Greenlanders* and *Eirik the Red's Saga*—are known collectively as the *Vinland Sagas*. Both sagas have an early thirteenth-century provenance, and it is likely that they were drawing on the same oral traditions. Although they have more similarities than dissimilarities, there are marked differences in style, approach, and sympathies. *Eirik the Red's Saga* is clearly the more sophisticated in its storytelling, but compared to *The Saga of the Greenlanders*, it sometimes appears hyperbolic and more tending to emphasize uncritically the deeds of Eirik's family, in particular his son-in-law, Thorfinn Karlsefni. Set together, these two sagas provide a reasonably credible history of the founding of Greenland and the discovery of North America. Where contradictions are apparent, it is the less glamorous detail of *The Saga of the Greenlanders* that is preferred.

Eirik accompanied his father to Iceland in the 970s, and there is a suggestion in *Eirik the Red's Saga* that both father and son had been forced to flee from the Stavanger district of Norway after being outlawed for declining to pay compensation for certain killings. Yet life in the far northwest of Iceland, where land was still to be had, was harsh, and Eirik's father did not long survive. Eirik, however, soon made a good marriage and took over the running of a farm at Haukadal in the more verdant southwest of the island. But before long, he was at odds with his neighbors. More uncompensated killings followed, and Eirik was obliged to leave the farm and take up residence on a tiny island at the head of the large western inlet of Breidafjord. His new neighbors resented his overbearing manner, and when they tried to contain him, they too fell victim to his vicious temper. Eirik was declared an outlaw and was forced to quit the country for three years.

Like many others, Eirik had heard the old stories of a new land far in the West; some Icelanders even claimed that in a certain light, from a certain vantage point, towering ice-capped cliffs could be seen far in the distance. With a return to Norway out of the question, Eirik gathered a crew and fitted out a ship. It would be a make-or-break expedition.

A four-day voyage eventually revealed that the towering cliffs were real enough, but, undeterred, Eirik pressed on down the coastline until he rounded Greenland's southern cape, where at last he sighted good harbor and green pasture. Here, not far from the inlet he called Eiriksfjord, he settled for three years. The almost unique 150-mile strip of green he had found was enough for him to name this massive glacial subcontinent "Greenland."

When Eirik returned to Iceland at the end of his outlawry, his report of lush land ripe for settlement was sufficient to encourage twenty-five ships to follow him to Eiriksfjord. Although bad weather allowed only fourteen ships to complete the crossing, this initial migration was sufficient to found a new community at what later became known as the Eastern Settlement (modern Julianhåb), so distinguishing it from the smaller Western Settlement (near modern Godthåb) that grew up near the more westerly coast to the north. In time, over two hundred farms were flourishing in the Eastern Settlement, with a further one hundred farms in the Western Settlement. A third settlement also developed midway between the two larger ones. At its height, Eirik's colony sustained in the region of five thousand settlers. Brattahlid, Eirik's own spacious estate, was the finest in the colony. As excavations have revealed, the main hall was some fifteen feet wide and fifty feet long. No longer did Eirik have to resort to violent extremes to ensure that he got the elbowroom his expansive personality required.

The Greenland settlers were well provided for from both land and sea, and their need for metal, timber, and grain was readily met by their export of subarctic animal furs, ivory, and falcons. Arduous and dangerous journeys far into the north, to the place that hunters called the *Norðsetr*, which lies between Disco Island and Kingigtorssuaq, could be rewarded with the capture of live polar bears, which fetched a high price at royal courts in Scandinavia. Despite the good living to be had from farming and fishing around the settlements, many Greenlanders clearly still retained that restless and questing spirit that characterized Viking adventurers, and medieval Norse inscriptions and cairns have been found hundreds of miles inside the Arctic Circle. It was this restlessness that Eirik the Red passed to his son, Leif.

Eirik the Red's Saga says that Leif had visited Norway as a young man and had been charged by the king, Olaf Tryggvason, to ensure the Christian conversion of Greenlanders. It was not an easy task, especially given that Leif's own father was the most obstinate of pagans, so much so that he was, at least for a while, prepared to stick to his principles and endure exclusion from the marital bed by his Christianized wife, Thjodhild. But, as was the case in Iceland and the Faroes, Christianity was a historical force that brooked no resistance, not even Eirik the Red's, and not long after the year 1000, Greenlanders, too, were building chapels and churches for community and private prayer, as was the case at Brattahlid. By the twelfth century, the Eastern Settlement boasted an episcopal see with a fine cathedral located at the main stead of Gardar, and in due course, Eirik's founding settlement accommodated twelve churches, a convent, and a monastery.

Leif Eiriksson may well have been the catalyst for this change of religious temper, but he himself is unlikely to have been the pious type. Adventure was in his blood, and perhaps it was a story he had heard when yet a boy that had fired his imagination, for according to *The Saga of the Greenlanders*, Leif's great voyage of discovery had a curiously undramatic precedent.

Brattahlid was commonly the place where merchants and adventurers met and told their tales of perils on the high seas and in strange lands far away. It is probable that one such was the Icelander Bjarni Herjolfsson. Bjarni's misfortune was to have been blown wildly off course whilst attempting to visit his father, one of the first to migrate to Greenland. On eventually sighting land, Bjarni very much doubted whether it was his intended destination. For five days he followed the shoreline north, noticing hilly forests, then flat woodlands, and finally glacier-topped mountains. Despite the protestations of his crew, who, at the very least, saw the chance of replenishing the ship's supplies, Bjarni refused to put ashore. Instead, he turned east, and four days later he duly arrived at the Eastern Settlement. This was his story, and "many people thought him short on curiosity," says the saga.[4] However, Bjarni's tale of a new world got around, and the curiosity of the young Leif Eiriksson was very much aroused.

It may well have been fifteen or more years later when Leif purchased Bjarni's ship and assembled a crew. It had been his hope that his father would join him, but Eirik was aging, and when he took a tumble from his horse, he declared that it was enough for him to have found the land in which he now lived. Leif followed Bjarni's crossing in reverse, coming first to the northernmost land and then sailing south. Unlike Bjarni, he put ashore at every point. Baffin Island, Labrador, and Newfoundland were most probably what Bjarni had sighted. But Leif went farther south. The question is, how much farther?

It is apparent from the saga that Leif sailed south beyond Newfoundland, down the Straits of Belle Isle and into the Gulf of St. Lawrence, and so toward the eastern seaboard of what is now the United States. The description of where Leif then put ashore has continued to provoke argument among historians:

> [They] sailed into the sound which lay between the island and headland that stretched northwards from the land. They rounded the headland and steered westward. Here there were extensive shallows at low tide and their ship was soon stranded, and the sea looked far away to those aboard ship. Their curiosity to see the land was so great that they could not be bothered to wait for the tide to come in and float their stranded ship, and they ran aground where a river flowed into the sea from a lake.[5]

It was here that Leif and his men decided to build "large houses," and the saga is quite clear why:

> There was no lack of salmon both in the lake and in the river, and this salmon was larger than they had ever seen before. It seemed to them that the land was so good that livestock would need no fodder during the winter. The temperature never dropped below freezing, and the grass only withered very slightly. The days and nights were much more equal in length than in Greenland or Iceland. In the depth of winter the sun was aloft by mid-morning and still visible at mid-afternoon.[6]

In addition, we are told that it was at this place that Leif's men found grapes. Taking into account the climate of about one thousand years ago, the daylight hours in winter, the southernmost point at which salmon are found, and the northernmost point at which grapes will thrive, the indications are that they were somewhere in the region of latitudes 41° to 42°— in other words, between where New York and Boston are now situated.

Assigning a precise location to Vinland is not, however, an exact science, and there remains the possibility that it could have been either further north or further south. Skeptics have even suggested that Leif did not find grapes at all and that the saga authors had simply misunderstood the word for berries. Nevertheless, supporting the saga's claim is Adam of Bremen's late eleventh-century history, which says that no lesser authority than King Svein Estrithson of Denmark recalled how "fine wine" from Vinland graced the royal tables during his youth in the first quarter of the eleventh century.[7]

Unfortunately, no archaeological evidence has yet been unearthed along the northeastern seaboard of the United States to allow us to draw any firm conclusions. Moreover, numerous forgeries and dubious claims have not helped in bringing balanced judgments to bear. The most famous of these distractions are the Kensington Rune Stone in Minnesota, which would appear to have been carved by Scandinavian settlers in the late nineteenth century, and, more latterly, the so-called Vinland Map, whose advocates still need to explain the traces of twentieth-century chemicals in its "medieval" ink.

While the location of Vinland is uncertain, what is absolutely certain is the presence of Vikings on Newfoundland. On the island's northern tip, at L'Anse aux Meadows, the ruins of a cluster of Norse-style turf houses, along with a boat repair shop and a smithy, provide ample evidence of the Greenlanders' determination to colonize the area and launch expeditions further south. This determination, however, would not outlast three decades. The problem was that, unlike southern Greenland, North America was already inhabited.

Leif returned to Greenland laden with grapes and timber, clearly unaware that there was considerable potential for trouble in his paradise. He took over the running of Brattahlid, and it is not told that he ever returned to Vinland. But others of Leif's family were either less burdened by domestic commitments or less comfortably off, and, in total, the sagas tell of three more voyages to the far west.

Leif's younger brother, Thorvald, was the first to make the crossing—with fatal consequences. Thorvald is said to have used Leif's settlement to search inland, where he encountered no human presence. Then he sailed northeast, perhaps to Nova Scotia, and set about exploring the eastern inlets where he hoped to settle. It was here that he encountered a handful of natives and, in typical Viking style, killed them, or rather killed all but one who escaped and later returned with a large band of followers. In the onslaught that ensued, Thorvald was struck by an arrow and died. Those of his companions who survived fled to safety, and, having loaded the ship with grapes, returned to Greenland.

The Vikings called any such natives—whether American Indian or Eskimo—*skraelings*, meaning "ugly, stunted and barbaric," but their contempt was ill judged given that they were looking to found a colony, for these indigenous peoples numbered in the tens of thousands. Thorvald's nemesis was probably devised by the Micmac, who had occupied the region for over five thousand years.

The second attempt to turn Vinland into a permanent colony was urged by Leif's widowed sister-in-law, Gudrid, whose first husband had died in an attempt to make the westward crossing. Her second husband, the wealthy Icelander Thorfinn Karlsefni, was not hard to persuade that he could succeed where his predecessor had failed. *The Saga of the Greenlanders* says he took with him a crew of sixty, including five women and assorted livestock, whereas *Eirik the Red's Saga* trebles this estimate. In either case, all went well for a while, and when the natives came to investigate matters, a degree of respect was shown by both sides. As a consequence, a lively trade developed between Vikings and Native Indians.

It did not last. When misunderstandings led to one of Karlsefni's men killing one of the native traders, a massive retaliatory force laid siege to the settlement, and Karlsefni had no choice but to put to sea. Growing doubts about the viability of Vinland were further added to when Karlsefni returned to Greenland and reported a disturbing encounter with a murderous uniped as he tracked northward from the abandoned settlement. With him on the homeward journey was his son by Gudrid, Snorri, the first child of European origin to be born in North America.

According to *Eirik the Red's Saga*, accompanying Karlsefni on his voyage out to Vinland was Leif's sister, Freydis. When Karlsefni tried to establish an outpost far to the south at the place he called Hóp and was beset by warlike tribes, Freydis sent terror through the ranks of the attackers by baring her breasts and slapping them with her sword. These appealingly heroic Amazonian antics are not, however, corroborated in *The Saga of the Greenlanders*, which gives a dramatically different account of Freydis's character and deeds. To begin with, Freydis's visit to Vinland is said to have been a completely separate enterprise from that of Karlsefni. In this account, Freydis dealt treacherously with her two Icelandic business partners, exiled them from Leif's camp, and then successfully incited her husband to kill them. She personally axed to death their womenfolk. As a consequence, on her return to Greenland, she was considered to be a disgrace to the family name, a scenario that one might well think to be the more likely.

No further attempts by Greenlanders were made to establish a North American colony, but both Greenlanders and Icelanders are known to have made regular crossings for many years to come, gathering that most prized cargo in treeless Greenland and Iceland, timber. One record from as late as the mid-fourteenth century tells of a Greenlandic vessel blown into harbor in Iceland stacked to the brim with timber from Labrador. As for the grape harvest, that may well have died a natural death as a consequence of hostile natives in Vinland and the gradual deterioration of the climate during and after the thirteenth century. If this was the case, as seems a reasonable speculation, it is a fitting metaphor for what took place in the Greenland colony in the centuries following the Vinland voyages.

The settlement of Greenland occurred during the Medieval Warm Period, a particularly favorable time for seafarers in the North Atlantic, as ice floes remained north of latitude 70° and therefore hundreds of miles north of Eirik the Red's green strip. So things remained for almost two hundred years, until the cooling began. By the late fourteenth century, the sea temperature may have fallen by as much as seven degrees. For the Greenlanders, the consequences were dire. The Western and Middle settlements soon became unsustainable, and in the Eastern Settlement, pack ice threatened shipping and the livestock began to die out. Worse still was the increasing presence of another group of settlers, the Eskimos.

These Eskimos had migrated east across the subarctic regions of North America and had found their way to Greenland during roughly the same period that Viking settlers arrived there. Yet during the warm period they kept to the north of the island, where their arctic hunting skills were best employed. As the ice moved south, so did they, until eventually they encountered the Norse settlements. Scandinavian sources are inclined to present these *skraelings* as subhuman aggressors against peace-loving Christians. The Eskimos had a different perspective.

In tales preserved in oral traditions and set down in writing during the nineteenth century, the Eskimos tell of the savagery and the stupidity of the people they called the *Kavdlunait*. It is in these tales that the real problems of the settlers are revealed, for it was not simply a battle of wills between two ethnicities; it was much more the almost willful inability of the settlers to adapt to their changing environment—an environment, needless to say, in which the Eskimo was perfectly at home. One illustration of this is the tale known as *Encounter of Kaladit with the Ancient Kavdlunait on the Ice*. When a gang of Norsemen rampaged into an Eskimo village and slaughtered the unsuspecting men and abducted the womenfolk, one warrior, Kaladit, survived and tempted the attackers onto the ice, whereupon "they lost their footing and fell on their backs, others sideways and some went tottering about."[8] Kaladit's perfect adaptation to the terrain then allowed him to take revenge, spearing one man after another and rescuing what remained of his family.

In the rivalry between the Norse settlers and the Eskimos, the efforts of the Norsemen could almost be regarded as comical were it not for their genocidal intentions. But, in the end, it was not the Eskimos that wrought the end of the Greenlandic settlements, but the failure of the settlers to learn from them. In matters of diet, the Norse settlers persisted for too long in trying to maintain their livestock rather than exploiting more effectively the rich harvest of the seas; in matters of dress, they continued to wear homespun wool in the Scandinavian mode rather than sealskins; and, whereas the Eskimos used every part of their sea catches for nutrition and warmth, the settlers wastefully discarded anything they considered uncommon.

By the late fifteenth century, the population of the Eastern Settlement had drastically declined, fewer and fewer ships managed to negotiate the ice-choked seas, and Eskimos thrived and multiplied in every direction. The imperiled community was all but forgotten in mainland Europe, although Pope Alexander VI wondered whether the episcopacy at Gardar still prospered "at the world's end."[9] Not until 1540, when an Icelandic ship sailing from Hamburg was blown ashore near the Eastern Settlement, was this question finally answered. On the beach, the captain discovered a long-deceased male, part clothed in homespun, part in sealskin, his knife almost worn away through constant sharpening. The settlement was abandoned.

Conclusion

Statues commemorating Leif Eiriksson's great discovery have been raised from Scandinavia to the United States. Bronze images depict him scanning the horizon in Trondheim, Norway, where one tradition has it that his epic voyage began; in Reykjavik, Iceland, the country of his birth; and in Qassiarsuk, Greenland, once the site of Eirik the Red's Brattahlid estate in the Eastern Settlement, whilst in America at least fourteen statues to Leif, from Boston to Seattle, celebrate the Scandinavian attachments of the many who migrated there in the eighteenth and nineteenth centuries. This is fitting, for Leif Eiriksson—fearless, curious, independent, and fortunate—embodied much that was to be admired in the Viking spirit and, by association, much that is to be admired about all those who have sought out new lives in unknown lands, irrespective of dangers and misfortunes. It is the essence of the pioneer that Leif Eiriksson represents, and, in this sense, successes and failures are merely relative when set against the sheer act of will that set the precedent.

There is much else to be admired about the Viking colonists that surged across the North Atlantic. In Iceland in particular, the intelligence and creativity of medieval Scandinavians was nowhere better articulated. Law and justice were precociously framed there, and the literary talents of saga authors have assured Icelanders a prominent place in the cultural history of the West. Yet it should also be acknowledged that the intrepid Viking character that opened up new lands, and with them new possibilities, also showed that self-same aspect that terrorized much of Europe. The brutal treatment that Vikings meted out to those who stood in their way or sought to frustrate their claims was the abiding memory of the Viking expansion for all who were not of their kind.

It is, then, with a paradox that this history comes to a close. On the one hand, there is a great deal of romantic inspiration to be derived from the courage and daring of the thousands who sailed out of the fjords in their longships with a do-or-die attitude. On the other, there is the widespread evidence of savagery and greed. Whichever image one might prefer, the other will not allow it to stand alone.

Notes

Introduction

Notes

1 Hilda Ellis Davidson, ed., *Saxo Grammaticus: The History of the Danes; Books I-IX*, trans. Peter Fisher (Cambridge: D. S. Brewer, 1996), 292.
2 Seán Mac Airt and Gearóid Mac Niocaill, eds., *The Annals of Ulster (to A.D. 1131)*, part 1 text and translation (Dublin: Dublin Institute for Advanced Studies, 1983), 329.
3 For a full assessment of the material and literary evidence, see Martin Biddle and Birthe Kjølbye-Biddle, "Repton and the 'great heathen army' 873–4," in *Vikings and the Danelaw: Select Papers from the Proceedings of the Thirteenth Viking Congress, Nottingham and York, 21–30 August 1997*, ed. James Graham-Campbell, Richard Hall, Judith Jesch, and David N. Parsons, 45–96 (Oxford: Oxbow Books, 2001).

Chapter 1

Recommended Reading

Davidson, Hilda Ellis. *Gods and Myths of Northern Europe*. Harmondsworth: Penguin Books, 1990.
Faulkes, Anthony, ed. and trans. *Snorri Sturluson: Edda*. London: J. M. Dent, 1995.
Jesch, Judith. *Women in the Viking Age*. Woodbridge: The Boydell Press, 1991.
Larrington, Carolyne, trans. *The Poetic Edda*. Oxford and New York: Oxford University Press, 1996.
Lindow, John. *Norse Mythology: A Guide to the Gods, Heroes, Rituals, and Beliefs*. Oxford: Oxford University Press, 2001.
Orchard, Andy. *Dictionary of Norse Myth and Legend*. London: Cassell, 1997.

Notes

1 Carolyne Larrington, trans., *The Poetic Edda* (Oxford and New York: Oxford

University Press, 1996), 24.

2 Francis J. Tschan, trans., *Adam of Bremen: History of the Archbishops of Hamburg-Bremen* (New York: Columbia University Press, 1959), 207–8.

3 H. M. Smyser, trans., "Ibn Fadlan's Account of the Rus with Some Commentary and Some Allusions to *Beowulf*," in *Medieval and Linguistic Studies in Honour of Francis Peabody Magoun, Jr*, ed. J. B. Bessinger and R. P. Creed, 92–119 (London: Allen & Unwin, 1965), 100–101.

4 Eljas Orrman, "Church and Society," in *The Cambridge History of Scandinavia*, vol. 1, *Prehistory to 1520*, ed. Knut Helle, 421–62 (Cambridge: Cambridge University Press, 2003), 421. Translated from M. Cl. Gertz, ed., *Vitæ Sanctorum Danorum* (København, 1908–1912), 83.

5 Larrington, *The Poetic Edda*, 12.

Chapter 2

Recommended Reading

Binns, Alan. *Viking Voyagers: Then and Now*. London: Heinemann, 1980.
Griffith, Paddy. *The Viking Art of War*. London: Greenhill Books, 1995.
Peirce, Ian G. *Swords of the Viking Age*. Woodbridge: The Boydell Press, 2002.
Siddorn, J. Kim. *Viking Weapons and Warfare*. Stroud: Tempus; and Charleston: Arcadia, 2000.

Notes

1 Translated by Andrew Wawn in Vésteinn Ólason, *Dialogues with the Viking Age: Narration and Representation in the Sagas of the Icelanders* (Reykjavik: Heimskringla, 1998), 141.

2 Magnus Magnusson and Hermann Pálsson, trans., *Njal's Saga* (Harmondsworth: Penguin, 1960), 203.

3 Translation in Paul B. du Chailu, *The Viking Age: The Early History, Manners, and Customs of the Ancestors of the English-Speaking Nations*, vol. 2 (New York: AMS Press, 1970, repr. from 1889), 541.

4 *Saint Óláfs Saga*, in Lee M. Hollander, trans., *Snorri Sturluson: Heimskringla; History of the Kings of Norway* (Austin: University of Texas, 1964), 245–537.

5 Seán Mac Airt and Gearóid Mac Niocaill, eds., *The Annals of Ulster (to A.D. 1131)*, part 1 text and translation (Dublin: Dublin Institute for Advanced Studies, 1983), 369.

6 Alistair Campbell, ed., with supplementary notes by Simon Keynes, *Encomium Emmae Reginae* (Cambridge: Cambridge University Press, 1998), 19.

7 *The Saga of Harald Sigurtharson (Hardruler)*, in Hollander, *Snorri Sturluson: Heimskringla; History of the Kings of Norway*, 577–663.

8 *The Saga of Óláf Tryggvason*, in Lee M. Hollander, *Snorri Sturluson: Heimskringla; History of the Kings of Norway*, 144–244, 220.

9 *Sturlubók* recension of *Landnámabók*, in Jakob Benediktsson, ed., *Íslendingabók Landnámabók*, Íslenzk fornrit, 1 (Reykjavik, 1968), 32.

10 *Hauksbók* recension of *Landnámabók*, in Jakob Benediktsson, ed., *Íslendingabók Landnámabók*, Íslenzk fornrit, 1 (Reykjavik, 1968), 33.

Chapter 3

Recommended Reading

Airt, Seán Mac, and Gearóid Mac Niocaill, eds. *The Annals of Ulster (to A.D. 1131)*. Part 1 text and translation. Dublin: Dublin Institute for Advanced Studies, 1983.

Campbell, A., ed., with supplementary notes by S. D. Keynes. *Encomium Emmae Reginae*. Cambridge: Cambridge University Press, 1998.

Keynes, S. D., and M. Lapidge. *Alfred the Great: Asser's "Life of King Alfred" and Other Contemporary Sources*. Harmondsworth: Penguin Books, 1983.

Swanton, Michael, ed. and trans. *The Anglo-Saxon Chronicles*. London: Phoenix Press, 2000.

Notes

1 Stephen Allott, trans., *Alcuin of York c. A.D. 732 to 804—His Life and Letters*. Letter 12. (York: William Sessions), 1974, 18–20.

2 Máire Ní Mhaonaigh, "The Vikings in Medieval Irish Literature," in *The Vikings in Ireland*, ed. Anne-Christine Larsen, 99–106 (Århus: The Viking Ship Museum, 2001), 99.

3 Michael Swanton, ed. and trans., *The Anglo-Saxon Chronicles* (London: Phoenix Press, 2000), Peterborough MS, 65.

4 Swanton, *The Anglo-Saxon Chronicles*, Peterborough MS, 71.

5 Swanton, *The Anglo-Saxon Chronicles*, Winchester MS, 74.

6 S. D. Keynes and M. Lapidge, *Alfred the Great: Asser's "Life of King Alfred" and Other Contemporary Sources* (Harmondsworth: Penguin Books, 1983), 85. 7. Swanton, *The Anglo-Saxon Chronicles*, Winchester MS, 104.

8 "The Battle of Brunanburh," in Richard Hamer, trans., *A Choice of Anglo-Saxon Verse* (London and Boston: Faber & Faber, 1970), p. 43, ll. 1–4.

9 "The Battle of Brunanburh," in Hamer, *A Choice of Anglo-Saxon Verse*, p. 43–45, ll. 32–36.

10 J. A. Giles, trans., *Roger of Wendover's Flowers of History*, vol. 1 (London: Henry G. Bohn, 1849), 256.

11 D. M. Hadley, *The Northern Danelaw: Its Social Structure, c. 800–1100* (London and New York: Leicester University Press, 2000), 300.

12 Hadley, *The Northern Danelaw*, 300.

13 "The Battle Maldon," in Hamer, *A Choice of Anglo-Saxon Verse*, 50–69.

14 Swanton, *The Anglo-Saxon Chronicles*, Peterborough MS, 135 and n. 9.

15 Swanton, *The Anglo-Saxon Chronicles*, Worcester MS, 148.

16 *The Saga of Harald Sigurtharson*, in Lee M. Hollander, trans., *Snorri Sturluson: Heimskringla; History of the Kings of Norway* (Austin: University of Texas, 1964), 577–663.

17 From Alfred's preface to his translation of Pope Gregory's *Pastoral Care (Regula Pastoralis)*. See Simon Keynes and Michael Lapidge, trans., *Alfred the Great: Asser's Life of Alfred and Other Contemporary Sources* (London: Penguin, 1983), 125.

Chapter 4

Recommended Reading

Nelson, Janet L., trans. *Ninth Century Histories*. Vol. 1, *The Annals of St-Bertin*. Manchester and New York: Manchester University Press, 1991.

Scholz, Bernhard Walter, trans. *Carolingian Chronicles: Royal Frankish Annals and Nithard's Histories*. Ann Arbor: University of Michigan Press, 1970.

Wallace-Hadrill, J. M. *The Vikings in Francia*. Reading, UK: University of Reading, 1975.

Notes

1 Janet L. Nelson, trans., *Ninth Century Histories*, vol. 1, *The Annals of St-Bertin* (Manchester and New York: Manchester University Press, 1991), 56.

2 Ermentarius, *The Life and Miracles of Saint Philibert*, excerpted and translated in David Herlihy, ed., *The History of Feudalism*, 8–13 (New York: Harper & Row, 1970), 11.

3 Nelson, *The Annals of St-Bertin*, 62.

4 Nelson, *The Annals of St-Bertin*, 55.

5 Jón Stefánsson, "The Vikings in Spain: From Arabic (Moorish) and Spanish Sources," in *Saga-Book of the Viking Club, Society for Northern Research*, 4:31–46 (London: Curtis & Beamish, 1908–1909), 33–34 (abridged).

6 Ermentarius, *The Life and Miracles of Saint Philibert*, 11–12.

7 Eric Christiansen, trans., *Dudo of St Quentin: History of the Normans* (Woodbridge: The Boydell Press, 1998), 16.

8 Jón Stefánsson, "The Vikings in Spain: From Arabic (Moorish) and Spanish Sources," 40.

Chapter 5

Recommended Reading

Cross, Samuel Hazzard, and Olgerd P. Sherbowitz-Wetzor, ed. and trans. *The Russian Primary Chronicle: Laurentian Text*. Cambridge, MA: The Mediaeval Academy of America, 1953.

Davidson, Hilda Ellis. *The Viking Road to Byzantium*. London: George Allen & Unwin, 1976.

Macartney, C. A. *The Magyars in the Ninth Century*. Cambridge: The University Press, 1930, repr. 1968.

Pálsson, Hermann, and Paul Edwards, trans. *Vikings in Russia: Yngvar's Saga and Eymund's Saga*. Edinburgh: Polygon, 1990.

Notes

1 The term *Varangian* may derive from Old Norse *várar*, meaning "men of the pledge" or "confederates." More generally, the term indicated Scandinavian origin. The term *Rus* may derive from the Finnish *Ruotsi*, which signifies "rowers," or it may derive from the Greek word *rusioi*, meaning "blonds." In written sources, *Rus* could signify any Scandinavian or Scando-Slav.

2 For this and above quotes, see Samuel Hazzard Cross and Olgerd P. Sherbowitz-Wetzor, eds. and trans., *The Russian Primary Chronicle: Laurentian Text* (Cambridge, MA: The Mediaeval Academy of America, 1953), 59–60.

3 Cyril Mango, trans., *The Homilies of Photius, Patriarch of Constantinople* (Cambridge, MA: Harvard University Press, 1958), 74ff.

4 Cross and Sherbowitz-Wetzor, *The Russian Primary Chronicle*, 65.

5 F. A. Wright, trans., *The Works of Liudprand of Cremona* (London: G. Routledge & Sons, 1930), 185.

6 Cross and Sherbowitz-Wetzor, *The Russian Primary Chronicle*, 84.

7 George Vernadsky, *Kievan Russia* (New Haven and London: Yale University Press, 1948), 42.

8 C. A. Macartney, The *Magyars in the Ninth Century*, 213–14.

Chapter 6

Recommended Reading

Barrett, James H., ed., *Contact, Continuity, and Collapse: The Norse Colonization of the North Atlantic*. Turnhout, Belgium: Brepols Publishers, 2003.

Jones, Gwyn. *The Norse Atlantic Saga*. London: Oxford University Press, 1964.

Kunz, Keneva, trans. *The Saga of the Greenlanders* and *Eirik the Red's Saga*, in *The Sagas of the Icelanders: A Selection*, ed. Örnólfr Thorsson, 636–52, 653–74.

London and New York: Allen Lane, The Penguin Press, 2000.

Rink, Henrik, trans. *Tales and Traditions of the Eskimos*. London: C. Hurst & Co., 1974.

Wahlgren, Erik. *The Vikings and America*. London: Thames & Hudson, 1986.

Wawn, Andrew, and þórunn Sigurðardóttir, eds. *Approaches to Vínland*. Reykjavik: Sigurður Nordal Institute, 2001.

Notes

1 J. J. Tierney, ed. and trans., *Dicuili: Liber de Mensura Orbis Terrae* (Dublin: The Dublin Institute for Advanced Studies, 1967), 77.

2 Gwyn Jones, trans., *The Book of the Settlements: Landnámabók*, in *The Norse Atlantic Saga: Being the Norse Voyages of Discovery and Settlement to Iceland, Greenland, America*, 114–42 (London: Oxford University Press, 1964), 118.

3 Magnus Magnusson and Hermann Pálsson, trans., *Njals saga* (Harmondsworth: Penguin, 1960), chap. 70, p. 159.

4 Keneva Kunz, trans., *The Saga of the Greenlanders*, in *The Sagas of the Icelanders: A Selection*, ed. Örnólfur Thorsson, 636–52 (London and New York: Allen Lane, The Penguin Press, 2000), 638.

5 Kunz, *The Saga of the Greenlanders*, 639.

6 Kunz, *The Saga of the Greenlanders*, 639.

7 Francis J. Tschan, trans., *Adam of Bremen: History of the Archbishops of Hamburg-Bremen* (New York: Columbia University Press, 1959), 38.

8 Henrik Rink, trans., *Tales and Traditions of the Eskimos* (London: C. Hurst & Co., 1974), 320–21.

9 Jones, *The Norse Atlantic Saga*, 71.

List of Illustrations

of Christ. Source:W. G. Collingwood, *Northumbrian Crosses of the Pre-Norman Age* (1927; repr.,Wales: Llanerch Press, 1989), 156, fig. 184.

14 The mid-eleventh-century sundial at St. Gregory's Minster in North Yorkshire. The inscription tells how descendants ofVikings rebuilt the church during the reign of Edward the Confessor.Photograph by Maria Arnold.

15 Western Europe in theViking Age. Source: *The Vikings in History*, 2nd ed., F. Donald Logan, © 1992 Routledge. Reproduced by permission ofTaylor & Francis Books UK.

16 Viking Age Russia. Source: *The Vikings in History*, 2nd ed., F. Donald Logan, © 1992 Routledge. Reproduced by permission ofTaylor & Francis Books UK.

17 Tenth-century Icelandic parliament. © Copyright the Trustees ofThe British Museum, London.

18 Viking Age Iceland and the Faroe Islands. Source: *The Vikings in History*, 2nd ed., F. Donald Logan, © 1992 Routledge. Reproduced by permission ofTaylor & Francis Books UK.

19 Greenland and the Eastern Settlement. Source: *The Vikings in History*, 2nd ed., F. Donald Logan, © 1992 Routledge. Reproduced by permission ofTaylor & Francis Books UK.

20 Vikings in North America (New England inset). Source: *The Vikings in History*, 2nd ed., F. Donald Logan, © 1992 Routledge. Reproduced by permission of Taylor & Francis Books UK.

21 Statue of Leif Eiriksson in Reykjavik, Iceland. Photograph by Peter van der Krogt.

Select Bibliography of Viking Age Studies

Brondsted, Johannes. *The Vikings*. Harmondsworth: Penguin Books, 1965.

Byock, Jesse. *Viking Age Iceland*. Harmondsworth: Penguin Books, 2001.

Christiansen, Eric. *The Norsemen in the Viking Age*. Oxford: Blackwell, 2002.

Clarke, Helen, and Björn Ambrosiana. *Towns in the Viking Age*. Revised edition. London and New York: Leicester University Press, 1995.

Ellis Davidson, Hilda. *The Viking Road to Byzantium*. London: George Allen & Unwin, 1976.

Farrell, R. T., ed. *The Vikings*. London and Chichester: Phillimore & Co., 1982.

Haywood, John. *The Penguin Historical Atlas of the Vikings*. Harmondsworth: Penguin Books, 1995.

Haywood, John. *Encyclopedia of the Viking Age*. London: Thames & Hudson, 2000.

Helle, Knut, ed. The *Cambridge History of Scandinavia*. Vol. 1, *Prehistory to 1520*. Cambridge: Cambridge University Press, 2003.

Jesch, Judith, ed. *The Scandinavians from the Vendel Period to the Tenth Century: An Ethnographic Perspective*. Woodbridge: The Boydell Press, 2002.

Jesch, Judith. *Women in the Viking Age*. Woodbridge: The Boydell Press, 1991.

Jones, Gwyn. *The Norse Atlantic Saga*. London: Oxford University Press, 1964.

Jones, Gwyn. *A History of the Vikings*. Revised edition. Oxford and New York: Oxford University Press, 1984.

Logan, Donald F. *The Vikings in History*. London and New York: Routledge, 1991.

Marsden, John. *The Fury of the Northmen: Saints, Shrines and Sea-Raiders in the Viking Age AD 793–878*. London: Kyle Cathie Ltd., 1994.

Ólason, Vésteinn. *Dialogues with the Viking Age: Narration and Representation in the Sagas of Icelanders*. Translated by Andrew Wawn. Reykjavik: Heimskringla, 1998.

Orchard, Andy. *Dictionary of Old Norse Myth and Legend*. London: Cassell, 1997.

Poertner, Rudolf. *The Vikings: Rise and Fall of the Norse Sea Kings*. London: St. James Press, 1975.

Roesdahl, Else. *The Vikings*. Harmondsworth: Penguin Books, 1987.

Sawyer, P. H. *The Age of the Vikings*. 2nd ed. London: Edward Arnold, 1971.

Sawyer, P. H. *Kings and Vikings: Scandinavia and Europe, AD 700–1100*. London and New York: Routledge, 1989.

Sawyer, Peter, ed. *The Oxford Illustrated History of the Vikings*. Oxford and New York: Oxford University Press, 1997.

Simpson, Jacqueline. *Everyday Life in the Viking Age*. London: B.T. Batsford Ltd.;

New York: G. P. Putnam's Sons, 1967.

Smyth, Alfred P. Scandinavian *Kings in the British Isles, 850–880*. Oxford: Oxford University Press, 1977.

Smyth, Alfred P. *Scandinavian York and Dublin: The History and Archaeology of Two Related Viking Kingdoms*. Dublin: Irish Academic Press, 1987.

Wilson, David M. *The Vikings and Their Origins: Scandinavia and the First Millennium*.London: Thames & Hudson, 1970.

Acknowledgments

The primary debt of any historian is to the work of other historians, and I am pleased to acknowledge this in the recommended reading for each of the chapters and in the select bibliography of Viking Age studies at the end of this book. I would also like to thank the following institutions and individuals: the faculty of arts and social sciences at the University of Hull for supporting my research; the library staff of the Keith Donaldson and Brynmor Jones libraries of the University of Hull, the Gower Street library of University College London, the Brotherton Library of the University of Leeds, the Rasmuson Library of the University of Alaska Fairbanks, and the British Library, London, for their guidance and professionalism; Peter and Fiona Norton for their excellent help in tracking down Viking artifacts in the north of England; Natalie Mason for her invaluable advice; Matthew Pateman and Philip Cardew for, as always, giving me their full attention; Angela Matthews for organizing me; and all my friends and colleagues at the Scarborough and Hull campuses of the University of Hull. Any errors of fact or judgment in this book are thanks only to me. Finally, nothing that I do is possible without the patience and support of my family, especially my wife, Maria. To her, all favor is due.

Index

The History Press

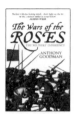   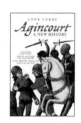

The Wars of the Roses
The Soldiers' Experience
ANTHONY GOODMAN
'A fascinating book' *TLS*
£12.99
0 7524 3731 3

William the Conqueror
DAVID BATES
'As expertly woven as the Bayeux Tapestry'
BBC History Magazine
£12.99
0 7524 2960 4

The Vikings
MAGNUS MAGNUSSON
'Serious, engaging history'
BBC History Magazine
£9.99
0 7524 2699 0

Agincourt: A New History
ANNE CURRY
'A tour de force' *Alison Weir*
'*The* book on the battle' *Richard Holmes*
A **BBC History Magazine** book of the year 2005
£12.99
0 7524 2828 4

Hereward The Last Englishman
PETER REX
'An enthralling work of historical detection'
Robert Lacey
£17.99
0 7524 3318 0

Richard III
MICHAEL HICKS
'A most important book by the greatest living
expert on Richard' *Desmond Seward*
£9.99
0 7524 2589 7

The English Resistance
The Underground War Against the Normans
PETER REX
'An invaluable rehabilitation of an ignored
resistance movement' *The Sunday Times*
£12.99
0 7524 3733 X

The Peasants' Revolt
England's Failed Revolution of 1381
ALASTAIR DUNN
'A stunningly good book... totally absorbing'
Melvyn Bragg
£9.99
0 7524 2965 5

If you are interested in purchasing other books published by The History Press, or in case you have difficulty
finding any History Press books in your local bookshop, you can also place orders directly through our website:
www.thehistorypress.co.uk